JOURNEY INTO POLAND

MY ROOTS IN GRANDFATHER'S VILLAGE

JANET HUDON HARTMAN

ISBN-13: 978-1508834977
ISBN-10: 1508834970

Dedicated to
My Grandfather

Acknowledgements

Having researched, travelled, and written this story over the course of so many years, it would be impossible to thank all the helpful people I met along the way. Little kindnesses are given freely and I'm assured our human nature is still intact.

I would never have reached my goal without my dear friend Gosia. She made it possible for me to move through Poland and sort things out while translating perfectly and without hesitation. I count her as one of my Guardian Angels.

My distant "cousin" Władek brought me deep into my family's history and local culture, and he too will be counted among my special and priceless resources. How dear he and his family have become.

Among my copy editors are my mentor since college, Ann Byrne, whose hand touched my manuscript not long before her death; and Lorraine Webber, whom I tormented through several versions of editing and whose patience and enthusiasm for the book energized me in the final weary days before going to press.

My family and friends listened, encouraged, and supported my travels, which must have been wearing.

And finally... my thanks to the universe for sending me all those feathers at just the right times. I know it was my grandfather sending me messages, urging me on.

Introduction

Finding my grandfather's village has been a long search, continuing through the advent of the computer age, the Solidarity labor movement in Poland, the dissolution of the Soviet Union (or fall of the Iron Curtain as I prefer to call it) and several journeys into a part of the world most Americans know little about. As my family history unfolds, I discovered many diverse methods of a genealogical seeker, the uncelebrated story of simple Polish immigrants and the remnants of the culture they carried with them to the United States. I had to peel away many layers before I reached the information I sought. For me, this was a long history lesson: lessons in geography, religion, politics, culture, and finally — in human kindness.

Years of researching census records and finding my way through cemeteries, immigration offices, handwritten journals and several trips to Poland — one of which took me behind the Iron Curtain in the early 1970s — all played a part in my decades long search for my family's roots. It has been a fascinating journey. Learning about the geography and culture has given me a greater understanding and appreciation of who my grandparents were and the lives they led.

My family story is peppered with both my mother's and my childhood memories, blending into the landscape of Poland's fields of barley and the enduring nature of her people today.

There are millions of similar stories to be told by other Eastern European families. Since the largest migration in history, around the turn of the 20th century and multiplied after World War II, thousands of people have attempted to connect with relatives who were separated from the western world by the restrictions of Communism and limited communication.

Many who search for their roots will be discouraged. Frustrated by stumbling blocks, they'll give up their quest. Hopefully the Zosa family story will offer other seekers the encouragement to keep going…to persist with the relentlessness of a true Pole – and find their grandfather's village.

Table of Contents

Memories

It was my first trip to Poland, travelling behind the Iron Curtain. Moving through the streets of Warsaw I was repeatedly struck by the faces of the people as they passed. I had never been presented with so many Polish faces before. My mother's family seemed to be evident in the face of every passerby. Few Poles lived in the neighborhoods where I grew up, and here I was struck by the homogenous nature of this country. Seldom did one see any other nationality. This was such a contrast to my home town and nearby City of Providence, known for its immigrant populations changing continually over the years. "These are my people," was all I kept saying to my husband. I had an overwhelming feeling of belonging to an entire city full of strangers – being part of them. Each man could be my uncle, each woman an aunt, or a cousin. I was so consumed by it all that I cried when we finally got to the airport, having to leave them and this magical place. That was the moment when I committed myself to knowing more about the Poles. I wanted to be with them, to share our history and absorb their culture into my life through my pores. It must be a genetic reaction to the cellular structure of the body to have such a strong effect on a person when experiencing a particular city, country, or culture that overtakes you like that. Some say it is a former life or karma that is responsible.

By the end of the tour I felt saturated with Polish culture which seemed so familiar to me and yet there was so much more to learn.

My grandfather was about five feet tall with a bushy moustache, a quiet step and a grin of approval that was warm and rewarding. Without a common language I can only relate the simple observances of a child who knew to look for that smile of acknowledgment. My grandparents were Polish on my mother's side. Simple people one might describe as illiterate and impoverished, to me my grandparents were an interesting part of my life – a Sunday afternoon opportunity to share good food and a visit with cousins in a fascinating place.

My mother, Amelia, and her siblings favored their father over their mother. I recognized that more and more over time. The family had good reason. That part of my story unfolds years beyond their death. Let me tell you about visiting the Zosas on Derry Street, in Providence, R.I. as I wrote the story for my mother on Mother's Day in 1979. (It's hard to find gifts for parents when they reach a certain age.) I decided upon the gift of remembrance for her, reaching back to my early years and Sunday visits to my grandparents. I read the story to her and my family on Mother's Day and tape recorded it as we spoke. I'm so glad I did that. Her voice is a treasure to me along with her comments, preserved beyond her lifetime.

Remembrance Story

On Sunday afternoons we visited my Polish grandparents in Providence. They never spoke English nor I Polish – but I enjoyed visiting them anyway. There were many things to study, observe, and explore. My Scorpio Moon (representing the detective in my astrology chart) no doubt began to exercise itself here in this foreign culture which was so strange and yet my own.

The day began with Catholic Mass at St. Peter's Church in Warwick, dressed in my Sunday best, complete with hat and white gloves. Dinner was more elaborate than weekday meals, probably because my working mother wouldn't have the time for a roast during the week: gravy, pickles, plenty of vegetables, seldom dessert, a cup of tea and a quick clean up. We'd pile into the old Ford and make our way to Derry Street in Providence. I knew the route well and would be excited as we crossed the bridge over the railroad tracks, turn at the mill, again at the yellow brick Nabisco building and on up the dirt road to the top of that very steep hill where the road ended at a fenced embankment. We'd pull off to the left and park beside Uncle Pete's Chevy coupe.

We entered the front door to a small dark hallway with stairs to the 2nd floor, an entry to the basement, and the door to my grandparents' apartment to the left. As soon as you stepped into that hallway and opened their door you knew you were in Poland. It was the smell. My grandmother would be sitting just off to the right beyond the television, and she would see my expression as I came through the door, taking deep whiffs of her golumpki (baked stuffed cabbage) – my eyes bright with anticipation. My mother would scold, "Oh no, Janet. You couldn't possibly be hungry. You just finished dinner!" Everyone would laugh. My grandmother loved it. She would of course heat some of her delicacies and I would of course be hungry enough to eat every bit. I think they really liked me for my Polish look and appetite. I was blonde with fat cheeks that always tempted a pinch, and I felt that I pleased these people, just by being myself.

Often my Aunt Agnes would be there at the same time with her family. She had three daughters – Dorothy the youngest was my age, Frances and Arlene were older, and her son Joey, whom we all thought so handsome, was her oldest, probably close to my sister's age, five years older than me.

Everyone would sit in the combination kitchen/living/dining room dominated by the big stove used for cooking and heating. It fascinated and angered me simultaneously. Fascinating because I hadn't known a stove that had to be fed coal to heat the kitchen and it had shelves on the backboard which seemed like a pretty handy idea. It angered me because it was always hot and my grandmother was never without burns and sores on her left arm. She explained that while she cooked she would smell something burning and realize it was her arm. She couldn't feel it and no one ever knew why. She never went to a doctor. Stubborn and fixed in her ways, she bore the inconvenience of keeping her arm in a sling using home remedies to heal the severe burns from wrist to elbow. Having no medical care and dreading doctors meant that whatever the ailments were, they remained undiagnosed until a near fatal moment. When the doctor was called, it was understood you were gravely ill. To resort to a hospital stay was to acquiesce that this would be a final move. One would not be expected to return home. Such was the level of understanding, fear, and economic stress.

Comfort is a relative thing, and I suppose one must weigh what one has against one's history. I always assumed the history was painful because there was so little discussion about the circumstances and living arrangements in the old country. In this kitchen/living room there was a 1920s enamel-topped table with wooden chairs. The knives and forks were kept in a cup alongside the salt and pepper on the table top. A number of straight wooden  chairs lined the walls with the radio (later a television) on the wall between the entrance and the pantry. Incidentally, I think they had television before we did. That would be because of Uncle Pete. He had a radio and television repair business; he was our version of high tech, and spent more time adjusting stations and reception than actually listening or watching. A collection of clocks were on the shelves and hanging on the walls. "Pa," as my mother called him, kept a watchful eye on them, comparing their faces to his pocket watch frequently; winding, adjusting, and fussing. Clocks chimed from the bedroom at the back corner of the house. That bedroom was my grandfather's, the master of the clocks.

Quiet most of the time, he was alert to the sounds of his clocks and would rise immediately upon hearing a bell or chime that wasn't exact. He tended the clocks always and was truly distracted only by a good belt of whiskey, which he would throw back toasting, "Na zdrowie!" and follow with a hearty clearing of his throat. His pipe kept him busy the rest of the time, like most pipe smokers, fussing to keep the tobacco lit.

The conversation drifted among Uncle Peter, Uncle Johnny (extremely shy and quiet), Agnes, and my parents in English and the Polish of my grandparents. I always knew the general drift of the conversation because of the expressions, tone of voice, and occasional English explanation.

There was another plain and sparse bedroom on that first floor and a dark pantry with a very old tin sink through which one passed to the toilet room – a minimal and rather dismal space. As a child I recognized a difference and that it was poverty, but all that was irrelevant. There was good food, fascinating people, clocks and a sense of an old world brought forward. The radio station played Polish music and had a Polish announcer. I was quite happy with it all.

Another joy was the yard. My grandfather had coops in the back yard. There were fences sectioning certain portions for the purpose of raising chickens, vegetables, pigeons, or whatever else he took a notion to nurture. I suppose it helped to feed the family during the depression. The twenty foot stone wall served as a back drop and privacy wall, the next houses and streets well above us. The pigeons had their home in old wooden boxes and platforms constructed by my grandfather to give them a place to roost. He fussed about his creatures and garden and was very clear with us to not disturb anything, but he was never harsh or scolding. One of his little sheds still stood in the corner of the yard in 1996 when I returned to photograph the house.

Cousin Dorothy and I used to run along the south side of

the house, careful to stay out of the garden and we'd sneak a peek in the kitchen window to see the adults. The family inside would laugh and point at these silly creatures who thought they were so smart. In retrospect I guess it brought a lot of joy to my grandparents. I still see their grins in my mind's eye.

Uncle Michael would stop in, handsomely dressed in his suit and tie, with Aunt Jenny and their children tagging along. His family was younger, so they didn't play with the rest of us cousins. When the entire family arrived, there weren't enough chairs so that much of the visit was spent standing. My Uncles Pete and Johnny stood at each side of the big stove, Uncle Mike by the door, and my handsome French father in his Sunday suit doing admirably well fitting into the Polish scene. Aunt Agnes' husband was rarely there and Michael's family kept their visits fairly short. I can't remember my father ever limiting the length of the visits. There probably were times when he would rather be elsewhere, but in my memory both my parents handled their obligations with grace and good manners.

The visits seemed to have the mixed flavor of duty and concern for family. It was an opportunity to exchange the news of each sub family group, the work of the week, accomplishments of the children, reports on home improvement projects. Peter told stories of his radio and television shop. Everyone had a job to complain about, a house to repair, and struggles with the prices of things. My grandmother would want my mother to braid her hair. She had wonderful, long chestnut hair, but with her paralyzed arm, she was unable to care for it properly. Living with Peter, Johnny and my grandfather, who wouldn't have a talent for braiding, she must have looked forward to my mother's arrival. Eventually her hair had to be cut short for practicality, which I thought was sad. Yet for all the urging from the family, she never did see a doctor about her arm. The choices were clearly made.

The priest came to the house to bless it on a regular basis.
I remember the family discussing it as an important event.
There would be palms at Easter season. Crucifixes and religious pictures were prevalent throughout my family's homes
on both sides of the family. I don't ever remember holiday
decorations or gifts in the house on Derry Street. If they were
there, it didn't mark my memory.

Neither of my grandparents ever drove a car, so they
were dependent on Peter and Johnny to do the shopping
and pay the bills. My memory doesn't extend back to my
grandfather's working years, but he had worked in silk mills
according to my mother. He developed severe asthma or
emphysema which went untreated as did my grandmother's
arm. It was hard for me to know if there was a basic distrust
of the doctors, a problem with language, or simply the lack
of money to provide medical care. Certainly no medical
insurance or retirement income was evident. Even at my very
young age it seemed curious. I wondered why no one simply
insisted and just delivered them to doctors. Yet I sensed that
even in their dependency, there was strength and resolve.
They were retaining their mastery of the family decisions.
Their adult children could argue and suggest, explain to them
and warn them, but they would ultimately decide for themselves.

There was clearly a respect for their choices, decisions,
and positions at the head of the family. This family, with an
uncelebrated history winding back across southeast Poland,
had made choices and decisions most of us would be far too
terrified to make. Aware of the hardships of immigrants at
the turn of the century, and realizing this was the man who
made the ocean voyage to the new world leaving his wife
and child behind; and this was the woman who boarded the
boat with a two or three year old son to follow her husband
to a new world; we can understand the strength of will and
the reluctance to argue with these decision makers. Although

1900s · · · ·

the hope of personal property and home ownership was nonexistent in their native land, these decision-makers had bought a home and raised five children here, speaking only in their native tongue. These were quiet people with mountainous determination. Who could argue with their iron will? So there it was. A family. There were three generations together on those Sunday afternoons. They shared simple pleasures, joys, shortcomings, differences, their age, their youth, and their culture. And in the memory of this little girl, they were all bound together in a sort of amber glow.

Memories flooded back as my mother (Nana, as we called her) listened to my descriptions on that Mother's Day. Her memories came in flashes as her mind skipped back through the years of her childhood. "Pa played a little accordion – [concertina]. [He] played Polish music. The Mazurka (Mazurek) was a favorite kind of music. There was a Christmas cradle song – like a lullaby. He played when he had time in the house after supper. When TV came out he couldn't believe it was real people [on the screen]." My mother spoke of her father fixing their shoes on an iron foot. "He put tacks in his mouth. Then he took one out and hammered them in all around the sole. Cut the sole out of leather. The immigrants did that at that time. They couldn't afford to keep buying shoes so they re-soled them. The next one (younger child) would use them." Her memories were random as they continued. "If ever I was fortunate to get a nickel that I could call my own, I would go to the store across from the school and buy a big fat juicy pickle. Not a chocolate bar. I would dig my hand right down in the barrel and pick a big fat one. Vinegar pickles.

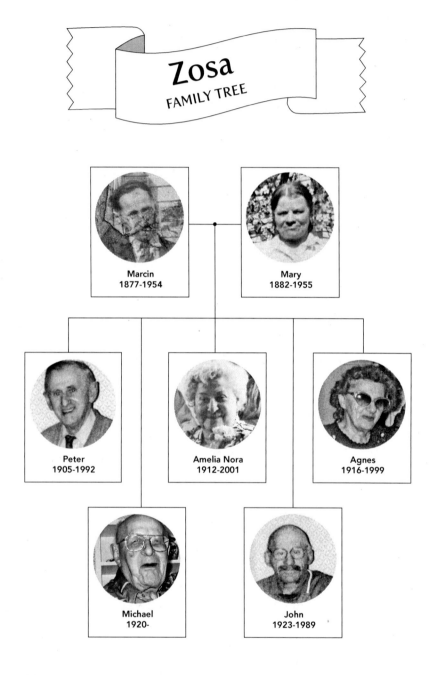

Zosa
FAMILY TREE

Marcin
1877-1954

Mary
1882-1955

Peter
1905-1992

Amelia Nora
1912-2001

Agnes
1916-1999

Michael
1920-

John
1923-1989

"Never any money so I never had a bike. That's why I never learned to ride. Couldn't afford skates. We made dolls out of clothes pins and rags. Most of the time was spent working in the house. Wash the clothes…on a wash board, no less. Wash the floors. Do the dishes. Once a week we took a bath in the round tub. Heat the water in the kettle − in the boilers, they called it. Coal in the stove to cook and heat the house. Had to clean it [stove] and blacken it every week. Called it the black bastard. So many years between us [kids] − we weren't close. On holidays the priest came to bless the house and the food on the table. I don't remember celebrating anything. No birthday cakes."

Nana's memories of Derry Street were significantly different from mine. She related stories of her grade school years, naming each teacher up to the 4th and 5th grade. I was astonished by the detail after having been told so many times that her childhood was too long ago and she couldn't remember. The stories continued.

"It was mostly Polish and Armenians on Whipple Street. There were some Lithuanians in the neighborhood, a few Russians, and a few Irish. The American Silk Spinning Company was at the bottom of Derry Street, where Pa worked on raw silk." She told of her father getting her a job in the mill. "The supervisor asked for my working papers and when he found out I was under 16 years old, he told me to leave and come back when I was 16. I later went back to the mill…earned $12.50 per week. I had to turn my money in [to the family]. I had fifty cents spending money and with my first fifty cents I bought myself a pair of silk stockings with a seam up the back."

These traces of memory were all that was available to us. My mother would share these few stories about her years at home with her family, but there was no information available about who her parents really were or where they came from. She usually cut the conversation short as soon as we began to ask questions.

Much of the family's history remained veiled behind an iron curtain not only of the Soviet Union's making, but involuntarily created by the circumstances of Polish immigrants struggling in a new culture, doing the best they could. The story of my grandfather's life has mystified and eluded me for years. I think of the quiet man and wonder where he came from. What gave him the inspiration and courage to move his family across the ocean to a world he never really understood? Few people spoke his language and he couldn't read a newspaper or sign, let alone a book.

I can't remember exactly when I began the search for my family's roots. It's been a curiosity that developed over time… like the way you develop a need for coffee in the morning. One day you know the day cannot begin without that quiet moment with a rich, dark roast. Questions about my grandparents grew right along with the size of my shoes. Those early memories developed into stark realizations as they grew older and I began to witness what poverty and death really looked like.

Grandfather coughed a lot, but black lung disease and other maladies that affected mill workers were unknown to us. He worked the silk mills where fibers flew through the air during the entire daylight shift − coating the lungs of the workers − accelerating their demise.

When I was 10 the family was called to the house on Derry Street. We learned that Pa had been visited by a doctor but had passed away in his bed after his final breathing struggle. Who knows if he could have lived longer with proper medical care? My mother was devastated by her father's death. She had adored him and wept often at the loss. A song, popular at the time, "Oh, my Pa-Pa" brought back memories and sadness each time she heard it. I witnessed all of the discussions, and the funeral, but was too young to fully understand more than the deep sorrow of everyone in Pa's family.

My grandmother was lost and totally disconnected from life after that. During family visits siblings talked about her grief, translating her Polish thoughts for her English-speaking family. She wanted to die, having no interest in living without her husband. She stopped caring for herself. Each visit meant more reports from Peter about her deterioration until she could no longer survive at home without attention. The siblings conferred, but without means, could do little to address the problem. Finally, against her will, she was hospitalized in an effort to find answers to her physical and mental decline. There were no answers to be found and she worsened daily. Ultimately she was moved to the state hospital for indigent patients. It was a cold, gruesome place where we visited on Sunday afternoons. My mother offered to bring something that might please her or ease her discomfort. I asked what her Polish response was. My mother said it was the same every time. "Can I bring you anything, Ma? Some Polish food, maybe?" "Bring me arsenic" would be her answer. She only wanted to die.

She hated the hospital — the care she got, the food. She stopped eating. Ultimately she decided to die on the same date as grandpa in the following year. She didn't make it — dying several days earlier than the anniversary of his death. That impressed me. I remember thinking what a strong will she had to make her heart stop beating because she no longer wanted to live without her husband. One year later I was gaining more understanding of death. It was my third consecutive November losing a grandparent: my father's mother in 1952 when I was ten years old, grandpa in 1953, and now my grandmother in 1954. All deaths occurred in November and all of them resulted in dismal Thanksgivings. At our house no radios could play for weeks; no fun, good times, or laughter were allowed. Those were my "formative" years. It's what I grew to understand about life – and death. The death certificates say that my grandfather died of Arterial Heart Disease and my grandmother died of "Multiple Myeloma." Both are buried in St. Francis Cemetery in Providence. There was little left behind to mark their lives.

> Story is both the great revealer and concealer. There is the story of what gets said, and the story of what remains unsaid. There is the story that covers up story. There is the blanket of silence thrown over the secrets, like people putting sheets on the furniture when leaving home. It's all still there, the shape of the lamp, the length of the sofa, the arrangement

1900s . . . .

of things on the coffee table, just cloaked, and in many ways revealed more definitively by the attempt to hide, the desire to protect.

The tension between what is said and what is not said is not just a peculiarity of my family. This is the dilemma of the human family. It takes courage to tell our stories. It takes belief that our stories will be received and held in respect.

Story Catcher, Christine Baldwin

The offspring now were left with no glue to hold them together. Each of the sibling's lives went in its own direction with emotional bruises of the past which would never heal, as I was yet to discover.

Years passed; families grew. My generation married; children were born. Some families struggled with welfare, children, and no husband. Many dramas unfolded but each family subgroup had enough to keep them busy and distracted until it seemed normal to be out of touch with the family. My mother continued to receive her recycled birthday and Christmas cards from her older brother, Peter. Uncle Mike & Aunt Jenny sent cards and occasionally there would be a phone conversation – rarely a visit. Aunt Agnes dropped out of sight totally for a period of time. My mother worried but said little about the long months when she knew nothing about her sister Agnes's life. My mother, Amelia, was a very private woman. When she mentioned her concerns, you knew it had festered inside for a long time. Part of her would have wanted it all to go away. She seemed to prefer forgetting about her family life, including her siblings' sometimes embarrassing behavior. I never knew what their childhood was like until I was an adult and little pieces began to fall from their hiding places. Quick glimpses were promptly stuffed back into a memory box which remained sealed and hidden as much as that strong Polish will could press it down.

We found a few scraps of paper with foreign words recorded by my father among his personal things after his death. Papa always tried to keep track of family details. He often brought us to see a distant cousin or an uncle on his French side of the family. He loved maps and globes and studied them for hours, trying to understand where someone came from. His primary school education limited him, but his natural curiosity kept him prodding, learning and stretching his abilities and knowledge in many ways. He spoke and read in French as well as English, but never learned the Zosa family's Polish. He would manage a few words or minimal phrases, but it must have been hard to have much of a relationship with his in-laws without a common language. Nonetheless, he tried to connect and understand.

My mother never learned to drive a car, but my father drove us dutifully to visit her family on Sunday afternoons. He evidently questioned my uncles and grandparents about their native village and he stumbled through printing the names that were mentioned in an effort to record the history of the family – if only in a primitive way. Although the scraps of paper held precious little information, they provided a beginning for my search into a culture we knew nothing about. Between the language barrier, minimal family stories, and the illiteracy of my Polish grandparents, you had a sense that they were hiding something. All their offspring expressed similar feelings over the years. There was mystery in their coming to the United States and about where they had come from in Poland. If asked where they originated, there might be three answers given at alternate times. My grandmother came from Galicia, Pa from Kolbuszowa (misspelled), or later the answer given would be Częstochowa (also misspelled). The family was asking questions but did not understand the political history of Poland. They might know some of the language but not the nuances of how things were expressed in Polish.

My search for roots was further hampered by Uncle Pete. Born in Poland, the oldest son grew into the position of head of household over time. Many daily needs and decisions were handled by him in varying degrees of efficiency. The barest necessities were provided, but it was evidently satisfactory and no doubt more than they would have had in Poland. Once the family had grown and left, a tenant on the 2nd floor of the house helped to sustain them. There were no Social Security checks or retirement income; Peter's radio repair shop and Johnny's auto repair income were needed to run the household.

Uncle Pete was a weird guy who learned enough about radios and TVs (a new invention) to open a repair shop. He lived with his parents until their deaths, as did my Uncle Johnny. Neither uncle ever married. Pete smoked stogy cigars and always smelled of them. He was one of those guys who told terrible jokes and thought he was very funny. He felt he knew more than anyone and also thought he was charming and loveable — often hugging us as kids — while we wished he'd keep his hands and bad breath off us. Peter did things like recycle greeting cards which had been sent to him by crossing out the name of the sender and popping them into a mismatched envelope to send off to my mother or my aunt for a birthday or for Christmas. Everyone shook their heads and laughed at his obnoxious ways, but he was tolerated since it was he who stayed at home and cared for his parents, even if minimally. Peter presided over the house, its contents and any documents or other remnants of the Zosa past.

None of us visited the house again after my grandparents were gone. I think my mother was relieved to leave the memories sealed within those walls.

Farm Work in Poland to Mill Work in America

In the early 1900s my grandparents and many other immigrants arrived in the United States from all over the world. They
were fleeing their homelands because of wars, threats of wars,
famines and poverty. The Industrial Revolution in the United
States had opened the flood gates for people to come for factory
work in the great mills springing up in New England. Fall River,
Massachusetts was a major mill town, producing fabrics and
clothing for the masses. This is where Martin, my grandfather
chose to try his hand at providing a better life for his family.
We were told his step-sister, Agnes Skowrok, had arrived in the
United States before him. It was unclear how Agnes had come
or if she had a benefactor. The idea of a step-sister confused me.

Perhaps Martin's birth father died and a 2nd marriage resulted in the last name of Skowrok. It was doubtful the relationship was the result of a 2nd marriage after divorce, as divorces were virtually nonexistent in the passionately Catholic nation of Poland. Martin was said to have had seven older brothers, all of whom remained in Poland. There was no available information about their names or their families. There were no sisters mentioned except for the one step sister, Agnes. These shreds of information shared by the elders found a place in the recesses of my mind. I developed my own collection of family data which remained concealed for later exploration.

With thousands of immigrants arriving from all over the world, there was turmoil in handling the bureaucratic processing at Ellis Island. Because of language barriers in their new neighborhoods, the newcomers often wound up with shortened or simpler versions of their family names. We knew the Zosa name had been shortened (Zosa isn't a Polish name), but were not certain of the true spelling. We knew that Martin came to the United States first, leaving his wife, Mary, and son, Peter, in Poland, sending for them when he had earned enough money.

Transportation across the ocean at the turn of the century was by ship. Overloaded they sailed with poor accommodations and little food, but with an abundance of hope and courage. I was told that when my grandparents arrived in the new world, they settled in Fall River where my mother Amelia was the first American born to the family. The journey continued, following work and housing opportunities, to the Rhode Island mill towns of Central Falls and Pawtucket.

The mills were constructed for one purpose and relied on water power. The owners managed their own businesses and the labor was supplied primarily by whole families, parents and children. Mill owners provided jobs, and controlled housing, schools, and stores in exchange for 60-hour work weeks. Conditions in the mills may have contributed to reasons the Zosas kept moving toward Providence and a better life. Having come from a country where life was full of hardships, one can imagine how Martin and Mary felt about raising their children to send them into the mills. Peter was around 11 or 12 years old, old enough for mill work and Amelia, my mother, would be nearing working age at 8 years old. It is conceivable that their exodus from Fall River and Central Falls to Providence offered the promise of greater opportunities and led to their decision to relocate the family once again.

At one point the Polish population of Central Falls was the third largest ethnic group in the city. Mary, my grandmother, worked in the J & P Coates Ltd. Company from England. It was a thread mill in Central Falls, a major provider of jobs at the time. Central Falls is a city only one square mile and just a short walk to the site of Slater Mill, birthplace of the industrial revolution. "This has always been a working class community," said Kathy Martin of Central Falls (interviewed for a *Providence Journal* newspaper story), whose grandfather came to the city from Poland around the turn of the century. "The ethnic groups used to be more isolated. The little French, Polish, Irish and Syrian enclaves that defined Central Falls in decades past are now largely gone. I still see working class people, some much poorer than we were, but still wanting a better life for their kids."

Providence Journal

As 1920 approached, Martin came to Providence alone. He was a boarder in Mrs. Augustine's six tenement house at the bottom of the hill on Derry Street. The family referred to the building as the "barrel shop" or "the box factory," since it was later transformed from a tenement house to a commercial site. The fourth and fifth children were born here – Michael in 1920, when my grandmother was 40 years old, and Johnny (the youngest) in 1924, when my grandmother was 44 years old. "Johnny was born in the barrel shop" was the way Agnes described the event.

At the bottom of Derry Street, separating it from Admiral Street, were the railroad tracks. The Providence & Worcester Railroad had begun operation in the mid 1800s and proved to be a boon to industries by moving goods faster than ever before. This may have been part of the lure to Providence, assuming there would be more jobs available. The railroad served the family as well by dropping coal on the tracks as the cars bumped along entering Providence. My mother remembered being sent down the hill to pick up coal from the tracks to be used as heating and cooking fuel. Immigrant families have always had to devise alternatives for their families' survival.

The Providence Directory of 1920 lists Martin Zosa, laborer, at 56 Derry Street. Mr. Harris owned and rented the house at the top of the hill on Derry Street and sold it to Martin around

1925. Agnes remembered Mr. Harris coming to the house to collect the mortgage payments. There were a number of Polish and Lithuanian immigrants living in the area at the time. Amelia was about 13 years old, Peter 17, Agnes 9, Michael 5 and Johnny approximately one year old. No doubt Martin was told of the neighborhood by someone of his native tongue who had lived in Central Falls with them. Fifty-six Derry Street was the third or fourth home for the Zosas in the fifteen years since arriving in America.

It was shortly after moving into this house that Johnny, the baby of the family, was treated for a birth defect, with what was then called "club feet." Without a family car he had to be carried on foot to the R. I. Hospital a couple of miles away, and was seen at the clinic. He wore a cast from his feet to his hips, making him heavier and awkward to carry. Amelia helped her mother make this trek; her mother spoke no English and was not able to carry the child that far. This was the only event I ever heard of the family taking advantage of formal medical care.

Amelia, as the oldest daughter, also accompanied her mother to the markets in Providence. She read the signs in stores and on buses for her mother. One would assume from these reminiscences that Amelia had better English skills than any of the other members of the family.

Agnes was called upon to write letters to Poland. She was evidently more skilled in speaking and writing Polish, than Amelia, who was preferred when English was required. A story repeated many times in the family was that Agnes wrote

to a cousin, Victoria in Poland for her father. The correspondence was difficult because Agnes said she had trouble reading
the "bigger" words in Polish and needed help in the translation. Evidently Victoria was the only contact in the homeland
with the ability to correspond. At one point the cousin asked
the Zosas to send a kerchief from America. My grandfather
reportedly bought one, although the expense was a problem,
since "things were quite rough during the depression," Agnes
remembered. The story goes that the cousin wrote back that the
kerchiefs were prettier in Poland. Martin was very upset and
said, "The hell with her." He refused to write and Agnes said
the correspondence drifted off after that. And that is where the
link to Poland was broken. It was just that simple. According to
family stories, my grandfather left seven brothers in Poland. He
was the youngest. Agnes and Amelia didn't remember hearing
their names. Communication and discussion of family in Poland
ceased.

On nearby Bush Street in Providence lived a family named
Gremba. Agnes remembered her father reminiscing with Mr.
Gremba about their shared time in the Austrian Army, where
Martin learned to speak some German. It was thought that after
being discharged from service, Martin married Mary and left for
the States shortly afterwards. No documentation of his military
service, their births, marriage, or immigration was ever shared
with their children or my father. The mysteries surrounding my
grandparents' origins seemed curious to many of us.

A Secret Revealed

There was a day in 1962 when I had some business in Providence and my mother decided to ride with me, waiting in the car while I made my brief stop. We parked at a State building adjacent to the grounds of Rhode Island College. I had never been to this place before. There were several buildings which housed government offices and children "of the state." I later realized the Department Of Children and Their Families was located here, and this was a holding facility where children were placed with foster families or returned to a more stable family environment. I was focused on my business; I hardly noticed anything other than the building I visited.

When I returned to the car my mother had a strange look. "I've been here before," she confessed. Her expression told me to pause. It was one of those instances that isolates itself in a pocket of your memory. A vibration comes through the air that says we are in a moment of timeless reality. It was a moment which would exist forever... in both of us.

The story unfolded. "When I was a little girl I was in here. My father couldn't take care of us." It was when her mother was gone again. She shared that her mother was an alcoholic who would have serious bouts with drinking and disappear for a while. My grandfather, Martin, was left to care for the young children while he worked long hours in the mill trying to support them. He couldn't do it alone. He had brought his children to the State home so that they would be housed, fed and safe until his wife returned from yet another alcoholic binge. My mother didn't fault her father whom she always adored, even though it was he who placed her in the orphanage or state school. There were children there of criminals, of deceased parents, from broken homes, and all other sadness one could imagine. The vision stunned me to silence. She would not have elaborated even if I had the presence of mind to question her further. Her story was brief. It was told because it could not be contained within her heavy-hearted memory. It needed a moment of light and air before being tucked away again in that secret darkened compartment where much of her childhood had been stored. She asked me to never tell anyone about the incident or her mother's behavior. We never discussed it again. There was finality to her request. I never disclosed her secrets until after her death.

I knew my mother did not have a happy childhood and that

her mother wasn't kind to her. She seldom discussed it, claimed she forgot how to speak Polish and had never told me any of the dreadful details of living with an alcoholic mother.

That secret memory awakened my curiosity about this family, but the investigation would have to proceed with sensitivity. Anything I could discover about them or their culture must be uncovered carefully. My search would move slowly and incrementally — with hesitations and breaks — while everyone absorbed and assimilated the information before exploring further.

First Trip to Poland

Behind the Iron Curtain

1974

In the decade following my mother's disclosure about having been placed in a State home, my life was filled. I married a Navy man (we called him Hoot), had three children and moved around the country. There was no opportunity to investigate the family's history. I dealt with the problems of being uprooted and moving our growing family from one home to the next on a very small budget. Ultimately we retired from Navy life, settled into a house in the village where I was raised, and my husband went to work for an airline.

It was 1974 and we were planning to fly into Poland for a four day tour that would alter my future. We made a quick decision to take advantage of an offer available to airline personnel. The trip, at $189 per person, included airfare, hotel, tours, and several meals. Hoot and I jumped at the opportunity with little knowledge about where we were going except that it was my family's homeland, and we would be venturing behind the Iron Curtain.[1] No one we knew could offer any real information or share insights about what we would find when we got to Poland. You must remember there were no computers or Google searches at that time. It was our usual blind faith and exuberance that carried us to this new adventure which simply could not be bypassed. There was a long wait for our visas to arrive. We needed a certificate of birth registration, different from the average birth certificate. I harbored secret worries about my mother's maiden name which could cause problems. Visa officials ask many questions. Time was getting short and there were no visas. We called our venerable Senator Claiborne Pell and asked for his intervention. Perhaps his office could influence the process. When a staff person checked and returned our call, we were told that the Soviet Embassy was not impressed with the Pell staffer's call. They couldn't care less about a U.S. Senator. That gave us a bit of a start, realizing who we were dealing with and what the attitude might be if we ran into difficulties while in Poland. No matter. The visas finally arrived and we were on our way...caution to the wind.

---

1 Iron Curtain is the term used to describe the boundary line which divided the communist Soviet bloc countries, including Poland, from the West, beginning at the end of WWII in 1945 until the end of the Cold War in 1991.

On boarding LOT Polish Airlines you are immediately transported into the culture of Poland. Flight attendants and passengers speak Polish all around you. English announcements follow the Polish...ours is the secondary language. Service was impeccable, friendly and elaborate compared to today's typical flight. Linens were used, along with dishware and flatware, as opposed to today's plastic forks and cardboard boxes for a simple lunch. Polish cold meats, head cheese, boiled eggs, very dark bread, wonderful chocolate, sometimes foods we didn't recognize, were interesting and delicious to us. Attendants circulated throughout our flight with slippers, hard candies, hot face cloths, and vodka straight up! Known as some of the heaviest smokers in the world, the plane sometimes reeked of the overpowering stench of Polish cigarettes. We were smokers ourselves in those days, but this tobacco must have been taken from a sour field and laid to rot before being rolled into those dreadful cigarettes. All this was part of the transport into a different culture, and we shrugged it off, enjoying the flight, the people and all things unique to Poland.

At the airport in Warsaw, we were directed to a large holding area where everyone's papers and baggage were inspected by guards in uniforms. We watched as they probed into peoples' bags, sometimes enjoying a brief glimpse at a sexy man's magazine along the way. There was no intention to rush. The guards had a threatening air about them, very gruff, serious, and appeared ill intentioned. Their Slavic language was totally unfamiliar to us. It could have been Polish or Russian to our

1900s · · · · · 1920s · · · · · 1960s · · · · · 1970s · · · ·

ears, so we didn't understand the problems some passengers encountered or why there were delays. It seemed like hours before my turn came, and I held my breath while my belongings were checked. Nothing of interest was discovered and I was quickly motioned through the door to the next holding area. Now separated from my husband, I imagined what I would do if he were not allowed through this simple but significant doorway! Minutes passed and he came through. Our knowing glances were all we dared at the moment. Our next instruction was to exchange currency. You had to exchange $15 American dollars for Polish zlotys before being allowed to enter the country. The exchange was 32 zlotys to the dollar, which we thought was fantastic. We knew things would be inexpensive on this trip, but we had no idea what the exchange rates would be. We were not the kind of travelers who studied and researched prior to a trip.[2] A few cursory questions and casual conversations were all we needed for advance planning. We knew enough to pack long underwear, however; it was March and we figured on snow: hats, gloves, and sweaters – that was planning enough.

On the bus ride to the hotel, it was immediately evident that the city was young architecturally. Communist style apartment buildings, stark and unadorned, lined up with business buildings, bleak and cold. There are no redeeming features to these 1950s-60s boxes and cubes. Built for utility, one's sensibilities could starve in search of grace or charm.

---

2 Note: Our perceptions and limited knowledge during this period were not always accurate.

We were housed in a hotel which was unpretentious and unadorned, but very comfortable. Our tour bus brought us back and forth on planned tours. We promptly inquired about transportation to the city center and whether we would be allowed to travel about freely. The desk clerk advised us that we were free to go out on our own. We had met a couple on the tour who spoke some Polish, so the four of us quickly found a city bus to carry us on a on a spontaneous mini expedition. Street cars gathered in the business district and we were "all eyes," trying to take in every detail of daily life and commerce in the city. Two things impressed us that day. One was the soldiers (or military police) walking the streets with big guns and leather boots. They never bothered us, but you were always aware of their patrolling presence. Shoppers and business people moved about without seeming to notice them, but these soft and sheltered Americans were unaccustomed to such intimidation.

The second impression that day was of a modest older woman carrying packages in the street. Our companion asked for directions to a bus stop; we had lost our bearings. The woman explained in Polish, but noting that we were Americans and obviously lost, she directed us to follow her. She took off at a speedy gait expecting us to follow, never looking back to check on us. We obeyed, keeping pace the best we could. Stopping at a corner, she turned to give us final instruction, pointing to a trolley stop where other people were waiting. We barely had the chance to thank her, when she promptly turned back toward our original meeting place and hurried off to her own destination.

1900s · · · · · 1920s · · · · · 1960s · · · · 1970s · · · ·

We were left stunned with the realization that this woman had just walked several blocks out of her way to help us and obviously thought little of it! This was my first and lasting lesson about the Polish nature. These people need only to hear of your need for help and they will extend themselves beyond what most of us would think of as acceptable limits. Thirty some years later, I still remember that woman and her act of kindness.

The next cold early morning we were taken to Old Town Warsaw. We visited the little museum at the corner of the square where they showed a documentary film about the city's past under Hitler's madness: the bombing that continued for days, followed by explosions and further devastation, until the city was left with little more than rubble. And then the persistence of the Polish spirit took on the work of rebuilding. They didn't clear debris and build new buildings. No. Their tenacity drove them to gather broken crucifixes and pieces of doorways, reconstructing from artists' drawings and paintings of the past. Methodically they worked to bring Old Town back to its original design and character. Here is where I strained to fathom the unique Polish soul. No matter how many times I've crossed that cobbled square in Old Town Warsaw amidst these reassembled buildings, I am in awe of this work of undefeatable persistence and patriotism despite years of foreign domination.

We shopped in a gift store on the square where a shop keeper ran next door to get another penny (grosz) to make my proper change, insisting on my taking every bit owed to me. You wanted to hug these people.

My husband, Hoot and our travel companions amused themselves on nearly every corner with black market currency
exchange. Eager for American money as the zloty had plum-
meted to virtually worthless levels, young Poles found an enter-
prising solution. There were men milling around every corner
and entrance to the tourist hotels. At first happy to go from the
official exchange of 32 zlotys to 1 dollar, you can imagine the
elation as the numbers increased to 100 to 1 and more! Some
American tourists referred to it as "Monopoly money." Always
glancing over their shoulders, they continued their game of
black market money exchange despite the danger. I tried to stay
clear of the "action" and cautioned Hoot to be mindful of how
tricky it could be to free himself from the bonds of those uniformed men with guns if he were caught. Surely everyone knew
what was going on, but this amusement was a once in a lifetime

delight which knew no bounds. Each day brought another challenge in the street — learning to barter for higher and higher rates. In the end we figured we probably left Poland with more money than we had when we went into the country.

The department stores provided another bit of education. Washing machines with wringers like the machines of the 1940s at home were still being sold. Shelves were nearly bare as more zlotys chased fewer and fewer goods. Shortages of coal resulted in shops with little to no heat or lighting.

People lined up in the streets waiting to buy apples. These were images that will live with me forever. This Poland, once considered a major breadbasket of Europe, was suffering shortages of great magnitude under the hands of Communism by the early 1970s. The ruling authorities mismanaged industry, production, and the economy. Independent farmers were without sufficient fertilizer, in addition to the parts to repair their machinery.

T. Lawrence Weschler's book, *Solidarity, Poland in the Season of its Passion*, gives us quotes from the people who endured the lines in the bitter cold streets.

"'These lines,' a woman says to me with a sigh, 'This is what kills our time. This is what wears us down – the time we waste in strategizing our daily lives. How you have to remember to buy bread on Thursday, because the line's too long on Friday, and that it has to be brown bread, because white won't last till Monday – all these tiny, petty details, cluttering up your mind until you don't have room for anything else.' Another acquaintance tells me she feels that the shortages are a

calculated strategy on the part of the government to wear
the people down, to slowly rob them of hope and enthusiasm. But a third person – a sociologist – feels that while the
lines started out as an inconvenience they are fast becoming
an institution 'It's not that bad,' he assures me. 'This is where
people meet, slow down, talk, exchange ideas on what is
happening in the country. And then, the miserable situation
of our economy changes the dimension of living – now we
take tremendous satisfaction in the smallest things. Just
finding two bottles of milk becomes an adventure. A pack of
cigarettes can make my day – it feels like a triumph."

Our tours were plentiful, however. Every effort was made to
entertain us and provide us with bountiful meals. In an effort
to please the American tourists, bottles of Coca Cola were often
placed on the dinner table, assuming it to be an American staple.
The most memorable dinner was served to us in an old country inn just outside Warsaw. It was across from the delightful
little cottage where Frederick Chopin was born. We sat in a
candle-lit room of the composer's house as a talented young
pianist played for us. Chopin's amazing music filled the room
along with the realization of where we were. After our mini
concert, we crossed to the inn, where tables were set for a five
course feast. We chuckled at the little glasses of vodka set in
front of each plate. We drank it straight down and continued
the merriment throughout the traditional Polish banquet. A
trio of musicians entertained us as we ate. They sang native
folk tunes, joking with their guests. Everyone was joyful until
that moment when one of the tourists asked them to play their
Polish National Anthem. The mood immediately dimmed, the

joy evaporated from their faces, as someone translated their response which was that they were not allowed to play their anthem. There were a few suspended moments as we internalized what that must feel like. All of us free Americans, never having experienced the oppression of a Communist dominated life, were momentarily silenced as the reality was absorbed. The musicians quickly moved on to happier tunes to pull us back to a party atmosphere, but the significance of the moment was not lost.

At the airport we watched the armed guards inspecting the baggage of the Poles who were leaving the country. One old woman had a large bundle wrapped in sheets and carefully tied. The guard tore it apart in his search and left her with a pile of disheveled personal belongings. There she was struggling and silent with kerchief and old cloth coat, looking so representative of Poland's current and long standing circumstance. I knew I wanted to be part of it all as my tears kept rolling out without the ability to do more than sympathize, remember, and internalize these images.

Another guard pulled my husband aside, directing him into a small, curtained booth for questioning. He later described the moment to us. Once inside, Hoot's back to the wall, he felt as if the uniformed man must be seven feet tall and likely to crush him at the slightest provocation. The gruff question in broken English, "You got Polish money?" My husband had, of course, taken a few zlotys for mementos, which we knew was forbidden. Polish money was not to leave the country. Looking the guard

straight in the eye Hoot answered, "No" as briefly and absolutely as he could muster, while his blood and breathing were
temporarily suspended in fear. There was no search, and he was
released to join me as we moved gratefully out of that sinister
check point separating us from Communist oppression and back
to freedom. No doubt we were probably not in the kind of danger we imagined, but when you are being directed by armed,
uniformed giants wearing big leather boots and watching the
gruff, insensitive behavior towards humble people like that old
woman – you have a moment of fear and appreciation for your
own free homeland.

I wanted to stay, to help, to know them better. That experience is probably what ignited my determination to do a family
search. I knew I would learn more about this country and these
people. It might take years to find enough time and information, but I knew I possessed that Polish perseverance in my
blood, and no hindrance would impede my purpose.

What a chatter box I was when I got home from Poland. My
mother was pretty surprised by my obvious and overwhelming
response to the country and its people. I think it stunned her to
realize that Hoot and I loved the trip and the culture as much
as we did, in spite of Poland's strained circumstances. Either
she had never heard such descriptions of the country before, or
she had suppressed every memory of all things Polish. We tried
to duplicate some of the meals we had on our trip, and I began
to notice more and more traces of Polish culture in the way
my mother cooked. Things I never noticed now had a history.

1900s · · · · · 1920s · · · · · 1960s · · · · 1970s · · · ·

I realized she carried ingrained customs which even she didn't identify as having anything to do with being Polish.

We returned to previous discussions about the family, and I tried to learn about her childhood, holidays, and her parents' story about coming to the United States. Her response was always brief. There were minimal stories, almost no real information, and the discussion would end with her saying she'd "rather not remember. There was nothing good to remember." I did learn that Easter in the Zosa household was more of a holiday than Christmas. She remembered the priest coming to bless the house every year – and the family enjoyed a ham dinner. It was unclear whether that happened every year or intermittently. "There was no such thing as a Christmas tree or decorations," no money for gifts, no memory of a happy holiday. Discussions always went from a shred of information remembered, to a sort of silent thump, thump, thump as the past was repressed, stuffed back into the box of unwanted recollection – hidden on a shelf, doors closed, discussion ended.

Solidarity – Pope John Paul II

As my family grew, I was scrambling to balance full time work, involvement in local politics, raising a family and finishing my degree as an adult student at the University of Rhode Island. There was no time left for family searches. I tried to incorporate some investigation of Poland and its place in world affairs into my studies. I followed the news reports on Solidarity, the labor union effort born at the Lenin Shipyard in Gdańsk. So much about the Soviet bloc had remained unknown to me throughout my life and schooling. As my interest grew, I realized how little the majority of Americans knew about Poland or its people.

Two books were instrumental in bringing me a greater understanding and perspective about Poles and the times we lived in. One was a book on how the Soviets and Americans perceive each other, *The Other Side*.[3] It discusses the limitations of text books, movies and newspapers on both sides of the Iron Curtain. The writer dissected both the American and Soviet use of misinformation during Cold War years. It gave me a greater awareness of why we knew so little about life in Poland. Here was an informed explanation for why there was such an aura of mystery about my Polish family. Americans had been programmed to believe that everything in the Soviet bloc was evil and to be feared. The picture painted by the media was that everything behind that Iron Curtain was devoid of culture, sunshine, fine architecture, or people who were just like us. The propaganda worked in two directions – a concept that hadn't occurred to me in my busy, and narrow little world.

Karol Wojtyła of Poland was elected Pope in 1978, taking the name Pope John Paul II. The world was shocked at this departure from a traditional Italian pontiff. Westerners could not conceive what this meant to the people of Poland. His pilgrimage to his homeland in 1979 gave hope and strength to those oppressed Poles – the extent of which they had never known. In this country which is almost totally Catholic, the enormity of a first Polish Pope's visit cannot be described or understood outside of their realm. Pope John Paul II delivered his historic address to the United Nations in 1979. As described in Pope John Paul II's biography, *Witness to Hope*, the speech contained:

---

3 *The Other Side: How Soviets and Americans Perceive Each Other*, Robert D. English and Jonathan J. Halperin, Committee for National Security, Washington, D.C. 1988

… a powerful diagnosis of the crisis of late modernity which was far deeper than the conflicts between East and West, between Capitalism and socialism, between rich and poor. It was a crisis of the very soul of humanity, and the core of the struggle was spiritual and moral. Without once mentioning the words "communism" or "Marxism – Leninism," the address was a bold challenge to the Soviet System and was understood as such. As former U.S. Ambassador to the UN Daniel Patrick Moynihan, who was present, noted, 'I can attest from having watched that the Eastern European and Soviet delegates knew exactly what he was talking about, and for once in that chamber, looked fearful rather than bored.'

The Church, from John Paul's point of view, made its most effective contribution to peace when it relentlessly defended and promoted human rights, of which religious freedom was the centerpiece.

The delegates to the General Assembly had listened to John Paul's address in silence. No one had wandered about the floor of the General Assembly, as often happened during normal business. However, they construed its meaning; the representatives of the worlds of power knew that they had been listening to a force to be reckoned with."

"The [Communist] regime didn't even try to keep pace with the Church symbolically during John Paul II's return to his homeland in June 1979. Victory Square, scene of many of the Polish communist regime's great public displays, had been transformed by government workers into an enormous liturgical stage for the papal Mass. From it, John Paul would address one million of his countrymen live and tens of millions more on radio and television. The centerpiece of the altar platform was a fifty-foot cross, draped with an enormous replica of a priest's stole reminding all present that they were witnessing a sacramental representation of Christ's

sacrifice on Calvary. Beneath the huge cross, where Mary had
stood faithfully by, was a replica of the Black Madonna of
Czestochowa. No Polish hero in Polish history – not King Jan
III Sobieski, not Tadeusz Kościuszko, not Józef Piłsudski – had
ever entered Warsaw as Pope John Paul II did on June 2,
1979. Here the Pope gave what may have been the greatest
sermon of his life which was punctuated with the crowd's
chanting rhythmically. 'We want God, we want God, we want
God in the family, we want God in the schools, we want
God in books, we want God, we want God....' Seven hours
after he had arrived, a crucial truth had been clarified by a
million Poles' response to John Paul's evangelism. Poland
was not a communist country; Poland was a Catholic nation
saddled with a Communist state. Poland's 'second baptism,'
which would change the history of the twentieth century, had
begun."[4]

News reports heated up with the formation of Solidarity
and the brave workers in Gdańsk. Americans found themselves
rooting for these foreign workers straining under unimaginable
conditions. Solidarity became a vehicle to study Polish life, customs, religion and politics. I absorbed the news like a sponge.
The Soviet Union's dysfunctional bureaucracy along with shortages of food and equipment in nearly every sector of the society
had frustrated the Poles to the point of revolt.

Without organization, weapons, money, supplies or leader-
ship, the situation had spiraled down until the country teetered
on the edge of starvation. When I read some of the reports, I
wondered how they could continue through the winter. The

[4] *Witness To Hope*; The Biography of John Paul II, George Weigel, New
York 1999, 2001

summer of the Moscow Olympics (1980) brought more stress with another rise in meat prices. "Many Poles felt their meat was being shipped to Moscow for the festivities, a suspicion which only fueled their anger. The meat price decree, issued July 1st, provoked a rolling series of strikes. The strikes would result in the Soviet government sending in fresh meat supplies, workers would return to work, and then the process repeated in the next town when news of the previous results reached them.

Tensions were high when the authorities decided to fire Anna Walentynowicz, a 51 year old female crane operator at the Gdańsk shipyard. She was popular among the workers who knew she was competent and had trusted their lives to her abilities daily. "In fury over such firings and the recent price increases, the workers put down their tools on August 14th and refused to be dislodged from the factory, their fortress. The next day the strike began to spread throughout the region. August 15th is one of the holiest days in the Polish Calendar – the Feast of the Assumption, and a day particularly consecrated to the Black Madonna of Czestochowa."[5] In Poland you will find every action is related to their passion over their religion which is inseparable from their politics. Every religious holiday and historic event is carried in their memory and acknowledged as they move through each calendar year. Celebrations, memorials, shrines and tributes are known to every citizen, which is the only way their culture, language and religion has survived

---

5 *Solidarity, Poland in its Season of its Passion,* Lawrence Weschler, New York 1982

during the many invasions throughout their history.

And so those bleak days of strikes, demands, military take-overs, imprisonment and national prayer continued. Wechsler's book, *Solidarity, Poland in its Season of its Passion*, with his personal account of that period clarified much of the Polish nature for me. Things I had observed during my trip to Warsaw in the early 70s now had context, and I was identifying a whole range of attitudes and behaviors as I started to internalize the emotion of my Polish experience.

Throughout all these news reports I came to grasp the bravery of the Polish people. In the face of overwhelming odds they held to their faith and stood their ground in peaceful resistance. It was not coincidental that Pope John Paul II had strengthened their resolve during his visit in 1979.

This Polish Pope gave unimagined hope to the men of Lenin's shipyard and all the people of Poland. It has always been this blend of religiousness and governance which must first be understood in order to understand the Polish soul.

Unsettled
1980s–90s

The Zosa Siblings

My father, Hervé, died in 1981 and my mother, Amelia, continued to live her quiet life in the old house on Fair Street which they bought in 1943. She and her siblings stayed in contact through greeting cards at Christmas and birthdays. Agnes settled into a more stable lifestyle, keeping in touch with her older sister, Amelia, by phone on a fairly regular basis. By now most of their conversations centered on health issues, but my mother seemed to feel better knowing where her sister was and maintaining a relationship with her.

I was surprised when I learned that my mother had invited her siblings to her house for a visit in 1987. She wasn't the sort of woman who was comfortable with entertaining anyone other than her immediate family. She lacked confidence that others would want to visit her, and she wasn't much of a conversationalist to entertain company. At certain times she did things with strong resolve, however, and this was one of those occasions. Something must have triggered her determination, but I never learned what that was.

With Peter as the driver and Johnny cleaned up from his usual greasy mechanic's clothes, they picked up Agnes along their way and made the long excursion to my mother's home in Warwick. It was about seven miles from Derry Street in Providence to Fair Street in Warwick but you would think it was a hundred. To venture out of "the city" was always a very big deal. Michael wouldn't come that day. I assumed he was reluctant to be in the company of certain siblings even though he and his wife, my Aunt Jenny, seemed to enjoy their occasional visits to my parents' home.

Amelia served tea and pastries as the group visited. Everyone was cheerful that day. It was an uncommon day in their lives. Their focus was on one another and the remnants of family associations that would always exist. No matter how far each path had swerved, there would always be that amber family chord connecting them. Aunt Agnes talked incessantly about her illnesses and dietary restrictions. Johnny sat silent as he always did. Peter rambled on about his car, how hard his life was without someone to cook for him and how many times he brought Johnny to visit Agnes for dinner. They laughed knowing he visited only to get a free meal. He and Agnes seemed to exchange meals for his driving her places she couldn't reach by bus. Like my mother, Agnes never drove a car. It was obvious the two of them were staying closer to one another than with the rest of the siblings. They could laugh at one another; their lives seemed similar. Agnes had been alone for years after her husband left. She didn't appear to have a close relationship with her kids after years of grinding poverty that would send her to live with men who would support her. Her strained circumstances no doubt accounted for her being out of touch with my mother for many months at a time. Her daughters struggled for their basic needs, having grown up hard and sometimes totally out of touch with both parents.

I visited with the Zosa siblings briefly on that day, took a few photographs (which they surprisingly allowed me to do) and left them to their unassuming little reunion.

These were precious moments, never to be repeated. Following that day each sibling perished in turn. It was their last Sunday afternoon together as siblings – as if my mother knew the importance of gathering them one last time. It was unfortunate that Michael had not joined them. He was unwilling to make the effort to be with his siblings. It might have been too painful for him or he feared some misery would repeat itself, compounding his inconsolable anxiety surrounding his childhood memories.

There was no special report about their meeting, no life altering news was shared, but I thought my mother seemed glad to have brought them all together again.

Uncle Johnny 1989

There was a time when I resented the custom of conducting a wake prior to a funeral. My father had brought me to so many as a kid, that by the time I was 16 years old, I revolted. I refused to attend another wake with him or with anyone else. I felt they were barbaric, disrespectful, and often hypocritical. I watched people behaving solemnly at the casket, and later telling their stories at the back of the room. The men went downstairs to smoke, sometimes to drink and compare notes on where each branch of the family was living and working. Women grouped themselves generationally according to family branches and spoke of their children. It was a time to learn who had gotten married or who never did marry. The distant relative who came to the wake in a particular hat or dress and behaved improperly was dissected. I remember a woman who would arrive in a very grandiose manner — blessing everyone in the room as she entered, as if she were a high priestess. There was much commotion and whispering each time she arrived.

It wasn't until I was much older that I resumed my attendance at wakes, realizing the ritual was as much for the family left behind as it was to pay respects to the dead. It's often the only way family members come together in this modern world of busy people and diverse lifestyles. We see cousins, uncles, and children grown to adulthood and parenthood. Life stories unfold. Old sadness is revisited, but many happy memories are shared as well.

Uncle Johnny died unexpectedly in 1989, the youngest sibling in my mother's family. Never married, extremely quiet, a simple man working as an auto mechanic with an uneventful life. Family gathered for the first time in many years. Children of cousins were introduced. Where had life taken all these people who were connected only by blood lines? You make promises to stay in touch; someone volunteers some information or a photo referring to family history. Of course nothing materializes and the entire event is forgotten within the week. Our lives are so disconnected now; we have no commonality.

How many times did my mother say as I was growing up, that she was never quite sure of her name or her birthday? Her family didn't celebrate birthdays as people do today. She was embarrassed to have been told she was born on one date and then another. We thought her parents remembered the day she was Christened rather than her actual birth date. Amelia was born at home on Spring Street in Fall River, Massachusetts. At the time, only the church kept records of births and baptisms. She spoke of her name as well. She was Amelia Nora Zosa at the time of her marriage to my father, but in childhood, she was recorded as Emilia. She and my aunt Agnes would occasionally mention that their last name had been changed along the way. Their lack of understanding the problems encountered by illiterate immigrants offered their imagination an opportunity to develop an explanation. Speculation was that the authorities changed the name upon arrival in the U.S. – or that the spelling was simpler this way. Darker thoughts would include a devious effort to remain anonymous – as if their arrival here involved an escape. I'm not sure these inferences would have been voiced to my grandparents, but I heard it more frequently after their deaths. It was as if the mysteries of missing information were cloaked in a darker robe each year. Perhaps the questions don't fully materialize until we're 30 or 40 years old. In their case, it was too late to return to the source and ask the question of your parents again. They may have been taught not to ask too many questions or that the memories those questions evoked were not happy enough to revisit. Whatever the deep truth, I can only conjecture — as the Zosa siblings did — but hopefully, with more accurate information as I learn more about their history.

As I started my search for birth dates and towns, I knew my first challenge would be to establish the correct spelling of our name and verify it with documentation.

I had been told there was a trunk or box on Derry St. "with papers in it." After the death of the elder Zosas, Peter was in charge of the house. He decided who would come and go. Since there was no monetary inheritance, there were no attorneys involved in the distribution of personal effects. If there were valuable possessions, keepsakes or important documents, it would be Peter who would stand guard at the door and no one had the stomach to challenge his offensive manner to intrude into their parents' domain. The house was left to all five Zosa offspring. There was no effort to change the status quo as everyone knew Peter and Johnny needed a home while the other three siblings had married and established themselves elsewhere. Years passed and Johnny met a woman whom he moved in with. Peter launched an effort to have his siblings sign off on the house, allowing him to retain full ownership. The siblings had grown apart; hard feelings and bad memories peppering their relationships. My mother wanted nothing more to do with the house or the family arguments. Phone calls came to lobby for her vote in one direction or another. She ultimately agreed to sign off if everyone else would. The transfer of ownership would require a unanimous vote. I can imagine the voting tendencies, but I was young at the time, so I will not testify to the circumstances, except to say that there was no consensus. The house remained in a deadlock. Peter maintained it. He paid the taxes and other bills. He controlled the portals through which no siblings passed. It was an impasse that deepened resentments and may have been the inspiration for Peter to dispose of "the box," "the papers," and any personal mementoes from the house.

I ventured over to Derry Street many years later in the naive hope that I could reason with my uncle to part with one of my grandfather's clocks which I hoped to give to my mother for Christmas. I knew she would have loved having something from her father. I was willing to pay him for the clock, any amount of money, even though I felt my mother had some entitlement. I parked on the hill beside Peter's car and went to the front door with mixed emotions. A large vicious dog jumped at the fence barking and growling with such menace that I was sure everyone in a two block area must have known that I stood at my grandfather's door.

There was no answer to my knock; no entrance to my family's homestead. No clock from my grandfather for his Amelia. Never would there be an access to "the papers in the box." My Aunt Agnes later told my mother and me that Peter described the day to her, knowing full well who I was and bristling "What the hell does she want!?" determined to retain the impenetrable barrier.

The Internet

Our family's first use of computers was with primitive models using a television as a screen. These early computers were marketed as toys for the kids rather than the sophisticated form of research and communication they would later become. We were introduced to this magical technology beginning with the Vic 20 and the Commodore 64. They would provide a very basic understanding of programming and a comfort level that we built on when we explored later systems.

My work in real estate brought me further into the world of computers in the mid 80s. I remember how hesitant we were, thinking something would break if we didn't hit the right keys. Children learned faster than adults during this time but computers were not yet commonly available in homes or offices, as they would be in the next decade.

My daughter Susan's work was with Reuter's International News Agency in 1984 to 1989. She was part of a team that introduced "real time information" to traders and government offices. It was a major breakthrough in connecting the world in a vital way. Technology took off. The world was shrinking. Although it was predominantly big business and stock traders and departments of the government that first recognized and could afford the information access — it was not long before many companies developed ways to use the new technology and ratchet American business up another level or two. It was a dynamic period of time. Like an explosion which was impossible to harness, the technology refashioned itself almost daily. The wide use of computers would mark a pivotal era in world history.

The advent of computers probably encouraged me in my family search more than anything else. I was introduced to a Family Tree Program which enabled the user to enter family members, their birth, death, marriage dates, photos and send the information off to the internet for others to discover and attach to the tree, perhaps discovering another branch of family. This fascinated me as it organized and simplified the building of a tree with just a few keystrokes.

I began to learn many ways to search as more organizations came online. Of course, there is the long standing Church of Latter Day Saints of Salt Lake City, Utah, with its reams of microfilm loaded with millions of families' data. So many libraries and ethnic organizations began to expand, get online, and feel the pressures as the number of genealogical researchers increased. There was renewed enthusiasm now that the computer age taught us that so much information could become available without leaving our desks.

The Fall of the Iron Curtain 1989

Probably the most meaningful development in my search was the fall of the Iron Curtain. Central and Eastern Europe took on a revolutionary attitude in the autumn of 1989, which ended in the overthrow of the Soviet empire within just a few months. Poland's political upheaval, stemming from the Lenin Shipyard strikes, served as instigation for peaceful revolutions in Czechoslovakia, Hungary, Bulgaria and East Germany. These revolutions changed the balance of power in the world and resulted in the total collapse of the Soviet Union. It was the end of the Cold War.

Poland, the first of the group from the Warsaw Pact to break from Soviet domination, created labor turmoil which led to the independent trade union, Solidarity, led by Lech Wałęsa, who became a major political force.

The elections on June 4, 1989, were like an earthquake and the victory of Solidarity went beyond all expectations. The new non-Communist government took office in September, 1989, and was the first of its kind in Eastern Europe. By the end of the year, the trend spread throughout Eastern Europe, resulting in the biggest change since World War II. The Warsaw Pact was officially dissolved in Prague on July 1, 1991, and the end of the Cold War was marked by officials, followed by the Soviet Union being officially disbanded on December 26, 1991. It was a whirlwind of previously unbelievable proportion.

The Iron Curtain was gone. Once that barrier was removed, it was as if flood gates opened. Now computers became available in Eastern Europe and old records were dusted off. There were new ways to share information, to discover the past. This loosening afforded westerners access to information which was previously thought to be lost forever. Now there was new hope for all those Jewish families who had been separated when they were forced to escape the Holocaust. It was exciting for the youth in the "eastern bloc" to find greater access to so many things which had been minimally shared in the past. First and second generation Americans could know and "see" the lifestyles, landmarks and faces of their family's past. Of course television and movies had shown us many views over the years, but those glimpses were dramatized. The media concentrated on major cities, political players, notables, Nobel Prize winners and newsmakers. The Internet exchange could be selective and private. Individuals could email one another – chat rooms and forums would spring up overnight.

Uncle Pete 1992

Uncle Pete was the next sibling to pass in 1992, and again the family assembled for the wake and church service. One of Aunt Agnes' granddaughters had lived on the 2nd floor of the old Zosa house so she offered stories about Peter's last years. Some members of the family were suspicious that Agnes and her granddaughter were mainly interested in what they could loot from the house and perhaps inherit the property somehow. The scavenger attitude was particularly sad given that the house was worth so little and the contents so meager. There was an element of truth in the suspicions, knowing the level of poverty and the lifestyle of a few of the clan. Some of the siblings and their offspring struggled out of poverty to create a decent life for their family based on a very strong work ethic. Others never seemed to lift themselves above their most basic needs. Life's circumstances and the inability to pull it all together left them at the mercy of life's winds, blowing them from one miserable circumstance to the next. I wondered about the vast differences in how the siblings grew, developed and aged. None of them had much of an education and yet there was a marked difference in the way they lived and raised their families.

After Peter's death the house definitely had to be sold. The issue languished until I had my attorney step in to help in the sale to an abutting owner. The location and condition of the property made it worth very little to anyone other than this man who wanted the additional land. The remaining siblings refused to share the legal costs with my mother who wanted it all finished and handled properly. The few dollars of profit from the sale were divided among the three survivors and the Zosa house was gone. I remember feeling sad about how hard my grandfather had worked to provide a home for his family and no matter how humble, it must have been a great source of pride to him. It was an amazing accomplishment for such a man from Poland, barely out of serfdom, illiterate, never having driven a car or spoken English. It was easy to see where the siblings with a good work ethic had learned their life's lessons.

Persistence

Because of my husband's work with U.S. Air (U.S. Airways) I was afforded the luxury of flying privileges, which I used in order to spend several days in Washington, D.C. each year for my birthday. I would celebrate by flying away to wander in the museums and enjoy the spring blossoms.

In April, 1996 my daughter Susan had a business trip scheduled to Chicago. I decided that I would change my destination from D.C. to accompany her to the "windy city," which I had never seen. We ventured in on the weekend prior to her business meeting to allow us time to explore the city. This offered me an opportunity to seek out the Polish Genealogical Society Museum at 984 Milwaukee Avenue. It was a bit off the usual tourist route, in a neighborhood that looked as if it had seen better days. I was expecting to see a Polish influence in the neighborhood – perhaps a Polish market filled with sausages, cheese and dark breads. My hopes wouldn't be met, however, since the Poles had obviously moved on.

Although everything I'd read about Poles flocking to Chicago during the great immigration led me to these expectations, there was only one building wall painted with a Polish message. Now worn with time, it was lost to the graffiti, debris, litter and remnants of other ethnic groups who currently occupied the neighborhood. We found the museum anchored in the midst of a transitioning community. We were two of a small handful of visitors that day. Darkened halls and low heat spoke of its struggles. There were display cases of military uniforms and medals, old documents, photographs and a small dusty exhibit of Chopin's piano and favorite stool (which always traveled with him)...set in a hotel room where he prepared for his New York City performance. A small library was maintained for researchers, but the materials were of no use to me. I had no known family located in the Chicago area and no real knowledge of Polish cities or the language. Their collection probably wouldn't help my search at that point. I chose a few little gifts from their modest museum store, left a donation and took information about their membership. I later joined the organization in order to receive their newsletters, which I looked forward to for news of organizations and societies expected to complete a book or online computer access to information such as Austrian army records, genealogical data or stories written about the history of a family. There was value to the visit. Each day spent learning about the culture served to motivate me to look further. Somehow I would find my answers in spite of language barriers and minimal family information.

A Statewide Historic Preservation Conference takes place every year in Rhode Island. Local preservation commission members from the cities and towns gather with professionals from the field and interested members of the community for a full day together sharing information. Guided tours of significant structures within the featured community familiarize us with the unique history of the town chosen each year. A member of the commission is assigned to lead each tour, taking their group by bus or on foot through neighborhoods of distinctive architectural style, a public building from another era, an old farm, mill building, or other significant site.

In 1996 the conference was held in Pawtucket, the home of the Slater Mill and the birthplace of the Industrial Revolution in the U.S. Parts of neighboring Central Falls were included. Robert O. Jones, one of my favorite tour guides, brought us through churches during a session titled "City of Spires." Many churches were built in the area because of the various ethnic groups who came to work in the mills. Each ethnic group wanted its own church with the mass spoken in its native language.

The Blackstone River supplied the water power needed for the mills, which meant industry could flourish there. Thousands of immigrants came to the region to gain a first foothold in their new country. Opportunities for unskilled labor requiring minimal language skills were plentiful. From Fall River, Massachusetts, along the Blackstone River, into Woonsocket, over the waterfalls to Central Falls, Pawtucket and down to Providence, industry churned its wheels, providing hope to thousands who came to find the American dream. The Zosa family was swept along with other waves of immigrants keeping the belts, pulleys and weaving machines clanging. As the spinning wheels turned, long days and weeks of work made it possible for money to be saved by my grandfather to send for his wife and son and later buy a piece of American soil and home for his family.

The Federal census of 1900 recorded only 1863 Polish Immigrants in Rhode Island but that population grew to 8158 in

Providence alone by 1920. Something in the city was drawing the Poles, and my grandfather was obviously carried along with the tide. Bishop Harkins of the Catholic Diocese created seven new Polish parishes to accommodate the growing immigrant population, one of which was St. Hedwig's at 569 North Main Street, Providence. The family attended St. Hedwig's church, where Amelia was married to my father, Hervé J. Hudon, in 1931. Agnes (grandfather's 'stepsister') Skowrok's daughter, Hazel, was their Maid of Honor. It was the church where my grandparents' funerals were held, and where the priest came from to bless the house on holidays. Michael and Johnny were born in Providence so their christenings must have been there as well.

Researching family history has a way of taking you in directions other than what you had anticipated. One little "aside" for me was a coincidence involving the Zosas' parish in Providence.

My daughter Susan, had an "over the fence" neighbor when she bought her first home in nearby Edgewood. Mr. Spears expressed interest in our Pawtuxet Village Association's quarterly newspaper with stories about its historic homes and local folklore. He mentioned living in Pawtuxet as a young boy in the 1920s as his father, minister of Asbury Methodist Church, was building his new church about a mile away. I interviewed

Mr. Spears for a story. He told me the senior Spears had been alerted to an ad which offered parts from a church being demolished on North Main Street in Providence, and managed to rescue some benches and stained glass windows for his Methodist church outside of Pawtuxet. The coincidence was that the church being dismantled was the Zosas' St. Hedwig's, and the Methodist church where the parts were installed is just about a mile away from where my parents lived for forty years. My mother was totally unaware of being so close to the pieces of St. Hedwig's when she and my father bought their Pawtuxet home in the early 1940s.

Again I returned to my search thinking there should be records of the Zosa family in their parish churches. If there were Polish priests recording their membership and births, the records would reveal their original name and birthplace. I questioned a local minister about church records, curious to know if my instincts were correct in expecting to find this family information. He told me the church records are carefully maintained and preserved as "they can be considered legal documents. The courts could subpoena them to verify age, marriage or death of an individual. If a church is demolished or a parish goes defunct," he explained, "the records return to the diocese and are kept in the archives."

I had no response from the priest at the Zosas' church in Fall River, so I decided to look at their last parish and work backwards. This opened another avenue of investigation. Researching their church might give me more insight into their migration to Providence as well as discovering their true surname.

I knew that when the Zosas' church in Providence was razed under the city's Urban Renewal Program, the records of the church were transferred to St. Adalbert's Church on Atwells Avenue in Providence, the Polish parish which became my uncles' church.

I sent off a letter to St. Adalbert's Church explaining the family's history with the Providence churches and asked for help with church records. Moss could have grown on my mail box while waiting for a reply. It didn't seem to matter if you offered money for someone to do the search; the churches simply did not respond. Could there be so many inquiries each week that a simple form letter or post card couldn't be sent to tell you what to do?

I thought it would be nice to make copies of the Mother's Day story I had written for Nana and give a copy to my Aunt Agnes. Nana didn't think anyone would care about the story — and that it would involve too much work. I insisted, so she dragged the book out from the bottom drawer of the desk under everything that had been piled on top of it. Suppressed memories buried, as always.

We planned to visit Aunt Agnes in Senior Citizen subsidized housing in North Providence and brought the story along for a Sunday afternoon visit. We took the elevator and walked down a long hallway to reach her small apartment, furnished by necessity. We sat at the modest kitchen table as I probed her memories. I was looking for anything that would help me understand the family and give me direction for further investigation.

For my grandfather, Martin, we had a birth year of 1875 and determined he was 30 years old when he married my grandmother in her 25th year. I wondered why they waited so long to marry and Agnes pointed out that she once asked her father. He answered, "Things were tough, and it wasn't that easy to get married. In Poland you asked permission from the authorities for a marriage to take place."

Agnes remembered that she and my mother were born on Spring St. and Summer St. in Fall River and Pawtucket but which child on which street and in which city? The family had moved from Fall River to Pawtucket and then to Central Falls prior to Providence. My mother said, "I remember visiting Pawtucket. That was the only family I remember...his half- sister. I don't remember living there."

The sisters repeated the story told to them that their mother and their brother Peter had been stowaways on a boat which caught fire and their papers were lost. There were no official documents for either one of them. I had a hard time believing a woman with a three year old son could "stow away" or that they could enter the U.S. without documentation. With stories like that, you shake your head, make a note and try to keep the stories flowing. No sense in deliberating, because these are the scraps which have become embedded and all that was known to them.

They reviewed their mother working in the Coats Mill while Pa worked the silk mills. Eventually Pa moved to Providence, living as a boarder at Mrs. Augustine's. They repeated the story of Harris, who sold the house up the street to their father, coming to the house to collect mortgage payments each month. Again, they amused me with their description of Johnny being born in the box factory.

Agnes talked about recently going to see her brother Peter at Derry Street and noticing the absence of her father's clock on the shelf. "I got rid of it," was Peter's only explanation. She said the crucifix was gone as well – leaving "only the old dishes from No. Main Street – they got with green stamps." There it was again. All the stories ended in the same blunt, dismal carelessness. It made me crazy but there was no way to change who we were.

Conversation, instant coffee, a pleasant visit. I think my mother was glad to have seen her sister. Agnes promised she would read my story and we went off.

Planning for Christmas church going, I insisted to my

mother that we go to the family's old parish in Fall River. She acquiesced and my daughter Susan joined us. Unfortunately the original church had a fire, destroying the entire building. Mass was in progress when the fire broke out. The parishioners managed to save the old Stations of the Cross, wall hangings of the Polish saints, the Black Madonna and other cherished pieces which were later installed in the new building built across the street. We learned this from a layman deacon whom we met after mass in the newer building. The choir and priest were quite impassioned and dramatic in their devotions. Everything was rather progressive from the attitude of the priest to women doing readings to altar-*girls*. The building, although modern and unappealing to my taste, had a floor plan which made everyone seem close to the altar and very personally involved. We all enjoyed the entire experience and my mother relayed the story several times on Christmas Day to each person she encountered. We were all glad she enjoyed the visit to her first parish.

The occasion gave me incentive to contact the priest for photos of the old church in addition to my current request for church records of the Zosas. I would eventually send three requests for information to the Fall River church. There was never an acknowledgement of my letters and of course not a shred of information about my grandfather's village in Poland.

Aunt Agnes 1999

My mother's only sister Agnes, had lots of sickness, hospi-
talizations, special diets, and many doctors. In June of 1999 we
learned she was in the hospital and about to have surgery for
a blood clot. We visited her at Our Lady of Fatima Hospital in
Providence the night before her surgery. My mother, Amelia,
struggled to walk the long corridors to her room. By this time
my mother's health was also failing. "Aggie" was glad to see us
and in very good spirits. Her daughters Frances and Arlene were
there along with Frances' "man friend," Bob. The conversation
was light and happy — even when Aunt Agnes said "if I don't
come back, just take all my things from the apartment and split
them up." She didn't appear morose or worried. She laughed
with her daughters about old boyfriends they had and there
were jokes about Agnes' outspokenness.

My mother was in touch with my Cousin Frances about
Agnes' progress. There were days of Intensive Care, then
improvement and a transfer to St. Joseph's Hospital in Providence for rehabilitation. Amelia bought an African violet as
she planned to visit her sister in the coming days. We heard
that Uncle Michael & Aunt Jennie had visited and found Agnes
walking with a walker, and although she didn't recognize anyone, everyone was hopeful for continued improvement.

Unfortunately, the call came to my mother that Aunt Agnes
had suffered a heart attack, ending her life. My mother seemed
to take this death harder than the loss of her brothers. Although

there were many years when the sisters were totally out of touch and there were few common interests between them, they were nonetheless sisters with shared memories of their childhood. As the two of them aged, they had developed a rhythm of phone calls to keep tabs on one another's lives and health, even when they were unable to visit in person. Neither ever learned to drive a car, so visits were limited to whenever I would find a day to take my mother to North Providence or, more to the point, whenever she felt up to dealing with her family's drama. Family matters are complicated sometimes. What appears to be happening in the moment is unavoidably colored by events of the past which may have nothing at all to do with today's circumstances. It's too complex for someone outside the family to fully understand, no matter how hard we try and empathize. Each meeting came with the baggage of the past piled all around the chairs we sat in and on the table with the coffee cups. It seemed more painful for my mother than for Agnes, to remember details of the past. Agnes had greater ability to remember, but it also had to do with my mother's not wanting to remember. Nearly all of her childhood was repressed. The native language had been forgotten; barely any acknowledgment of where she came from ever entered the day-to-day life of my mother.

And so when Aunt Agnes died, it was another abrupt shove, as if someone opened a door my mother was standing behind and nudged her back in time, reopening the memory box, exposing wounds once again.

As had become a habit now, my mother, my daughter, Susan,

and I attended Agnes' wake. It was a time when you could expect all the family members to turn out. Now there were only two siblings left to the old Zosa family, my mother, Amelia and Michael. Most of the room was dominated by cousins, some of whom needed to be introduced to one another because life had taken this extended family in such different directions. Susan and I "worked the room" as is our nature, but Uncle Michael's family sat remotely with invisible barriers surrounding them. They disliked and distrusted Agnes' family and had trained their children not to speak to anyone in the family. Unfortunately they continue that behavior to this day. I cannot remember one conversation I ever had with those cousins. A wake seems to bring out these family divisions. People come to pay their respects out of a feeling of duty to their family, but not necessarily because of a fondness for the people in the room.

One cousin from out of state was ostracized because others disapproved of her life decisions while another cousin's son was surrounded because he was on the "favored" list. Now there was another layer of family in the next generation that had been born and grown into adulthood in our estranged family. The more social members chatted and enjoyed getting to know one another, sharing stories about the intervening years and what they remembered of Aunt Agnes. Now we could exchange emails and try to renew relationships, but with nothing more than blood lines in common, the inevitable happened – everyone drifted off into their own separate lives.

Pieces to the Puzzle

As the world became more proficient in the use of our new computer technology, there were more and more creative programs designed. I discovered an excellent plan which the City of Hamburg put together. This would be a boon to the millions of families and genealogists reconnecting with their families separated by WWII and the Iron Curtain. I wondered if it would include my grandfather's voyage. The project description deserves to be repeated here in its entirety.

The Hamburg Project

An enormous project has begun in May 1999 at the State Archive of Hamburg: in the course of four years the personal data of 5 million people, who emigrated via Hamburg from 1850 to 1934, will be digitalized and gradually made available for inquiries on the Internet.

Making all this possible was a partnership between the public and private sectors. The software and hardware was made available by Debis, Oracle, Siemens, as well as Sun. 25 disabled employees will enter all data as well as answer any inquiries made via the internet. Employees involved will be remunerated by the State Welfare Office, with financing protecting the handicapped by law, stemming from a number of corporations not having fulfilled their duties toward this law.

Beginning in the winter of 1999 the first period of years

starting with 1890 should partially be accessible on the Internet. The entire scope of data can be accessed for a fixed charge as well as the issuance of a certificate. In the long term these charges should be used to secure some of these working places permanently. The city of Hamburg, accommodating emigrants in the past and to this very day, is in exclusive possession of lists of those who passed her utilizing the harbor. Even though Bremen and other cities lost almost all these precious lists, only Hamburg managed to safeguard complete records covering the flow of emigrants from 1850 to 1934.

What makes these lists so valuable is the fact that even the hometowns from whence the emigrants stemmed is recorded. Anyone researching a family tree will treasure this crucial factor.

Even though the American multiple-volume Glazier/Filby reference work "Germans to America," covering US immigration from 1850 to 1890 is available, the very large error margin due to faulty reading as well as other drawbacks are the basis for numerous justified complaints by researchers in this highly specialized area. Opposing that, the Hamburg lists include German emigrants in addition to the millions of other nationalities, mainly from Eastern Europe.

A very difficult financial situation made long-time Hamburg plans to digitalize the immigrants lists quite tedious.

Thanks to the Internet, the first phase of emigrant lists from 1890 to 1914 will be made globally available at the present. The decision to primarily offer the above time period coincides with the fact that the lists, albeit with errors, covering the period 1850-1890 had already been set up by Glazier/Filby. Furthermore, most emigrants passed through Hamburg 1890 – 1914.

According to plan, in the year 2003 the city of Hamburg will be able to display the lists for the entire period covering emigration from 1850 – 1934.

The Hamburg State Archive is the source and safe-keeper of all emigrant lists stemming from this period as well as all Hamburg history. All the data pertaining to the emigrant lists is processed and brought to the Internet, here at this center. Any help needed by anyone accessing this information, will be tended to by one of the 25 well-versed people, specialized in reading this material and waiting to help.

As of winter this year the Hamburg archives will offer Internet access to the first round of years. With this facility in place anyone looking for that "special" ancestor will successfully be able to do so.

Taken from "Hamburg to Amerika" website

The Internet as well as the creative thinkers of Hamburg were going to be a boon to so many thousands of families. I wished I knew for certain if my grandfather had come through Hamburg. I still wasn't even positive of the Polish spelling of his name.

The RI Historical Society Library has a long tradition of maintaining family information for genealogists. My initial interest was to visit their facility on Hope Street in Providence in order to find information about a very old RI family with ties to Pawtuxet Village. Many hours were spent copying old diaries and scouring volumes to gather all that I could on the distinguished Bowens of Providence.

While in the library, my eye fell upon the census books of Providence for the years around the 1930s when my grandparents came down from Massachusetts and into Providence. I searched several volumes to glean home addresses and family names listed in the census of 1920 and 1930. Sometimes there would be no listing or certain family members would not be included. It may have been the fault of the census taker or the person who answered the door or another tenant in the building providing the information. I imagined the reluctance of my grandparents to answer the door to an English speaking census taker, clipboard in hand. Having come from a place invaded by foreigners who wished to annihilate your language, religion and culture....and having no English skills themselves ... I imagine the meeting would have been uncomfortable, and as brief as possible. If one of the kids translated for the parents they might not include everything...or names could be misspelled. Nonetheless, it was exciting to me whenever I found even a trace of the family's history recorded in some old volume which might not be touched for years, but was there to be found by some curious grandchild long after the members listed were gone. A remnant of their lives...testimony in this revered institution that said something about those plain undistinguished lives. This was a trace of my family's existence. While wandering the stacks I took the opportunity to scour the old marriage record books of Providence to find my parents' marriage recorded there.

The library's collection includes many volumes, microfilm, donated documents and more that I would someday love to find the hours to explore. The Historic Society library is a brick building, c.1822, where you ring the bell to enter. Hours of operation are posted on the front door. Once inside, signs instruct the visitor to leave all personal carrying cases, handbags and coats in the hallway where lockers are provided. You sign in before entering and are greeted by a librarian who can direct you to your needs and give instructions on how to use the collections. Closely monitored, but available for only your donation and special care, it's a small charming assemblage of RI heritage.

The Society developed a web site and began the arduous task of inputting data for greater public access to their archives. A directory of cemeteries came online as a result of a project started in 1990, which has attempted to identify every pre 20th century grave in the state. It can be accessed through a link in the Society's web page. It takes many hours to input all the data. Judgments must be made as to which items are the most useful to the greatest number of searchers. Obviously it becomes prohibitive to include everything contained in the collections. There will always be a need for personal visits to these institutions for a more complete review of their archives. Their web site at http://www.rihs.org/resref.htm can acquaint you with the availability of information, hours of operation, contact persons. I love to visit these precious old book rooms.

As the Internet became more popular there were more groups developing sites that related to genealogical research. One such creative approach was a site titled "Random Acts of Genealogical Kindness" developed in 1999.

You decide to volunteer to do a bit of research at a local newspaper, cemetery, library or church near your home for someone in another country or state who is unable to visit that location. They request something specific; you do the local leg work and either email, fax or mail the requested data to the searcher. In exchange, you post a request on the site's listings, stating your need. Another volunteer in the location of your interest will in turn respond to your request. Some people answer multiple questions or complete multiple requests because they are so deeply involved in this type of research activity. For some it has become a hobby — almost an addiction.

I assisted others with our local cemetery records or I referred them to the RI Historical Society website and phone number. I explained the closeness of adjacent towns in our small state, and the way people moved across those town lines which may have been non-existent in the years of the researcher's quest. We don't have to go many generations back to find "pre-township" status for some places in Rhode Island which were not officially established in the 1800s.

I did the best I could for several seekers and found help in

my search for another branch of our family, for which I was grateful. Since I was still uncertain of many details regarding the Zosa family, I could not create a question for this site.

As time moves on and I become more certain of the spelling of the family name, I might re-visit "Random Acts" for help with other family connections. The use of the site is free and can be accessed at www.raogk.org.

One of the volunteers who helped us with another family exploration brought us more joy than she will ever know. She searched her local newspaper's obituary columns in a small town in Alabama. The paper's archives were unavailable online and we had no response from written requests. The volunteer's visit to the library and the death notice gave us a great deal of infor- mation. Fortunately the paper gave ample space to each death notice – probably because it was such a small town. All family members were listed, as well as pall bearers for the funeral, the name of the church and last known address of the deceased. That was huge. An entire branch of the family tree became evident in one broad stroke. When you have lived with so many questions for years it can be an overwhelming feeling to sud- denly be given such a wealth of information. It floods your brain as you re-calculate your history. Suddenly there are connections between these members and others in the clan. Pieces fall into place with a flutter of fulfillment. I can scarcely hope to com- municate what this could mean to people who never got to know a parent, grandparent or sibling.

Nana, as I preferred to call my mother, was an avid reader. Her day always included reading the newspaper and scanning the Death Notices. She would alert me to familiar names and sometimes she'd find names from the past which would jog her memory and help me with our Family Tree. She had found a few notices which included the names Czeczot and Borek.

In October of 1999 I decided to try contacting two persons listed in the local phone book, who might have some connection to us. I wrote to A.D. Czeczot and Lawrence T. Czeczot of Providence. When Nana saw the names she suspected they were related to the family that sponsored her father when he first came to Fall River. I was hopeful that someone could give me a shred of information which might offer a clue to get me from Fall River backwards to a town in Poland. My letter included several family names which I hoped would enable the reader to verify our relationship.

Nana and I revisited the conversation a week or two later. Oral histories don't roll out in a continuous fashion – but rather with starts and stops. I hoped I wasn't tormenting my mother who found it difficult to remember things. Forgetting an unhappy childhood means losing the good memories as well. We went back to a Death Notice she had found earlier for Michalina A. Borek who died at 53 years old – widow of John Borek, Sr. How was this name connected to all of our family discussions? Well, Michalina was a sister to Sophie, who loaned my mother her wedding veil when she married. Sophie was Mrs. Sophie (Skowron) Flower of Central Falls. (At one point I thought the name was Skowrok.) Michalina was my mother's bridesmaid at her wedding. Sophie and Michalina's mother was Agnes Skowron, married to Albert Czeczot. Agnes was the "step sister" who sponsored my grandfather when he came to America. The step-sister was always described as "a tiny woman born with a club foot who wore a high laced shoe with a big heel." That snippet of memory would later help me to identify a key family member.

In that same season, I followed my mailing with a call to Ann Czeczot. She was living in senior citizen housing in Central Falls. We spoke briefly and she verified our connection in the family. She was one of those people who is uncomfortable talking on the phone for a long time. She didn't want me to drive my mother up to meet with her, but she promised to have a friend drive her to meet my mother and me at my mother's house in Warwick. It would have to wait for better weather and for her friend to have free time. Although I would have gladly driven to connect my mother and me to a part of the family that links us to my grandfather's arrival into this country, it was obviously not going to happen any time soon. We exchanged Christmas cards and I sent a copy of the family tree for her to examine, but there would never be a meeting. I think my mother was as disappointed as I was. She might have enjoyed reminiscing with someone from that part of the family. She had been close to Hazel, who was part of her wedding party, and of course, Sophie who loaned her the veil.

The families might have remained close if transportation had not been such a problem. When my grandfather moved his family further south from Fall River and Central Falls to Providence, it was difficult to continue their visits. So many of them never drove a car, and without that, it became too expensive and cumbersome to visit people living as far away as Central Falls – a mere 5 miles away. When my grandmother was drinking and disappearing for days or weeks, my grandfather had neither time nor money for social times, I'm sure. The two branches of the family did stay in touch somehow, at least until the time of my mother's marriage in 1931. Each marriage meant dividing leisure time with another branch of family. Children demanded still more attention. Working mothers meant even less time for family relationships outside the immediate nucleus. And suddenly the years are gone, along with the closeness of the cousins.

On Nov. 11, 1999 my phone rang and the man on the other end identified himself as Larry Czeczot. He had received my letter which I had sent into the wind never knowing if I would have success in making a connection. You have to be ready when these calls come from out of nowhere in the midst of your busy life. First thing is to grab for pencil and paper. He knew from the details of my letter that we were part of the same clan. His grandmother was Agnes, whom he verified did have a bad foot with one heel higher than the other. Telephone conversations with Larry followed. He always wanted to call me rather than my calling him. I took notes as quickly as he spoke. He helped me piece together his section of the family tree (he remembered my Uncle Peter smoking his stinking stogy cigars) and promised that we would meet or talk some more soon. I mailed a copy of the family tree as I understood it, and later sent a Christmas card, but received no response. I had a clear sense that he didn't want me to call his home when his wife was there. Not wanting to disrupt his privacy, I didn't try again. Often I have found that family members are momentarily intrigued by this research and connections to other members outside their immediate circle, but often that interest is short lived. Everyone continues with their own lives with little or no time or inclination to be associated with their extended family.

As I prowled the Internet looking for ways to continue my research, I checked into Ancestry.com. Within Ancestry, I searched old census records for Massachusetts and Rhode Island. Birth, Death and Marriage records are also available through this wonderful resource, but nothing was helpful to me. My family seemed to run under the radar.

Ancestry.com leads you to FamilyHistory.com within the site. They described it as "an Online Genealogical Community." Here there were message boards where I posted family names, but the responses came from others who were looking for information about their own families. They had no connections to offer me. I saved the messages from other seekers in the hope that someday I would find the link that would connect everyone. I kept thinking about my family saying that my grandfather mentioned leaving about eight brothers behind in Poland. Maybe other brothers came to the United States after the family was out of touch, or the children of those brothers could have come to the States. The seekers on the message boards could be my cousins or second cousins, but how could we know without that crucial information contained in a complete family tree?

A forum I found online within <u>Delphi.com</u> was a brilliant concept to connect people from around the globe. It became the platform for one of my most priceless discoveries. The site allowed individuals to set up a forum on any subject for free. The site billed itself as "the ingredient in successful web communities that bring people together."

There were a variety of options within Delphi. You could discuss a range of topics from romance to recipes, but the section that interested me involved forums for genealogists with a specific section for Poland. I checked into the Polish Roots Genealogy Forum and found people from all over the world trying to find the secrets withheld during the Cold War years. The Delphi Forum offered an opportunity to find the answers to many questions.

Internet access and personal computers were slower to arrive in Poland. There were those who were fortunate to have computers at their office where they could occasionally log on for personal use. Others would go to the little Internet Cafes that were springing up – sometimes only one or two per town. However the new technology and access to the western world was such a draw that they managed a way to include the time and costs in their budget.

A few key people were committed to the Delphi Forum and eager to help all those seekers from around the world connect to their country of origin. Someone from the U.S., Australia, or Canada would post a query about a town in Poland, a family name, or a translation and whoever picked up the message on the other end would try to find answers or they might give leads about where to look for the answers. We connected with others who had the same questions or who were a few steps ahead of us in the genealogical search. It was a fabulous way to share information and sympathize with other families who had been disconnected over time and wars.

I searched everyone else's questions and discussions and came to realize there were vast numbers of us with the same problems connecting to earlier generations. Often experienced genealogists checked in to clarify points or to give instructions on where to find records. Repeatedly, I read about people trying to establish an accurate family name and town, while Poles on the other end of the message-stream tried to find answers in their old maps, telephone books, or other resources. The messages were interesting reading and helped me feel part of a larger community with Eastern European roots, all of whom shared my frustrations because of a lack of family data or understanding of their Polish heritage. The internet was introducing us to one another.

Our numbers mushroomed overnight as people accessed the internet throughout the world. Those who knew more about searching government records came in to the forum to assist beginners. Translators were kept busy as well as historians who could tell us what happened to records during and following World War II.

It became more obvious that the Catholic Church would be crucial to any search. Yet people complained of not getting an answer when they wrote letters to a church...even when a donation was included. Warnings went out not to send money in an initial inquiry. We could not trust the Polish mail services and didn't know if our letters were getting to their destinations.

During Poland's many years of being occupied by other countries, the Austrians claimed a section of southern Poland, which they renamed Galicia. Some names of towns were changed as well. When I learned this, I realized I needed to know more of Poland's history and geography if I was going to find grandfather's village. My father's notes said my grand-mother was from Galicia.

When the Austrians invaded, it became mandatory for all young men to serve three years in the Austrian Army. Martin would have been eligible at the time. I had been told consistently that my grandfather served in the Army and foolishly thought this would be a logical place to find information about him, his family and home town. I started posting questions about the Austrian Army in the Forum. With the Austrians' reputation for accurate record keeping, one could assume these records would be a reliable resource. I learned that all the servicemen were interviewed annually for pay purposes and a kind of census taking. Records would show a man's age, marital status, last home address, parents' names, occupation, etc. After inducting these young men and collecting the data, the armies later stored the information in a location which today could be in a different country. As I learned more about Poland's history and the impact on daily life, I came to understand the complications of my illiterate immigrant grandfather trying to explain his past to Americans who knew so little about Polish history. (Few people in the U.S. know Poland's story even today, never mind when Martin Zosa came to this new world.)

What seemed like a gold mine became another disappointment. I didn't know grandfather's correct name. I had no idea which years he served in the army or which home town name was accurate. If only I could get past that first step, which was to verify his correct name and his village.

There was talk of the Austrian Army records going online soon. I was thrilled that such a project would come to fruition for all the thousands of families trying to connect with their ancestors. I needed to discover the true family name in order to be ready for this new opportunity.

I posted various questions about towns and family names culled from scraps of paper left by my father who had been curious about his Polish in-laws' origins. He had noted their responses to questions about where they were from and spelled the words out phonetically. I first learned about Częstochowa's

Black Madonna when it was mentioned in one of his notes.

Pajęczno was another town mentioned in my father's notes. I learned it was just north of Częstochowa. All indications were that grandfather was from that region.

No one ever recognized the family name of Zosa. A Ukrainian woman here in the States conjectured that the name could be Ukrainian because of the vowel at the end. That rule would then apply to my grandmother's maiden name of Wieluba. My notes saying she was from Galicia could mean she came from the section which was part of Ukraine.

Under "Surnames" in the forum, I posted a message under "Name Endings." When the Zosa name didn't produce results, I thought of my grandfather's sponsor and step-sister with the surname Skowrok or Skowron. I found postings about the name Skowronek and posted a message under "Altered Polish Names." Soon I was receiving messages from others with that name or a similar version trying to make a connection in their family tree.

My postings were discovered by "Niki Fory" on the other end of the internet, and it was the absolute best day of my entire search to date. I had no idea if it was a man or woman answering me, but the challenge of discovering the proper spelling of the name must have intrigued my new pen pal.

The first response was to clarify the questions re: Skowronski, Skowronek, Skowrok and Skowron. Then on the question of name endings, I received the following email from Nikifory on November 11, 1999.

"All I'm guessing about how the Immigration officials shortened or altered Polish names is by observing how difficult
it is for foreigners to pronounce some Polish words (with
complex consonant clusters). I would assume that whenever
a name was changed at the Immigration's, it was to simplify it
by deleting some of the consonants – eg.'szcz' (pron. SHCH)
could be simplified to just 'cz', and the spelling altered to 'ch'
in order to render the approximate pronunciation. I believe
simplification was the most common pattern.

"About Zosa, it doesn't look like anything Polish apart from
that Zosia would be the Polish diminutive of Sophia. The suggested Rząsa ('Rz' pron. as ZH like in the French word 'jour',
and ON as in the French 'bon') with the first 'a' having a little
comma attached to it. Zhonsa, so it would be quite close to
Zosa. I have no other explanation. The best way is to research
your relatives – perhaps they remember how your grandfather himself pronounced the name (then I could help you out
with the likely spelling).

"About Wieluba, it can be Ukrainian and/or Polish. If Polish,
then I would associate it with the South, which is exactly
where Częstochowa is."

I immediately knew I had a valuable resource. Here was
someone who knew how to sort out the linguistic challenges
which plagued so many of the American descendants of Polish immigrants. I was over the top with joy. Of course I ran
to my mother with my news. She was always amazed at how
much was happening with this new technology. She found it
hard to believe anyone would care about sorting out this family's history and was incredulous that I would find someone in
Poland who could help me. When I asked her about how her
father pronounced their name she said she thought it could be

as Nikifory had explained but once again she deferred to her sister Agnes for Polish pronunciation. She consistently told me she had forgotten her Polish. Evidently family members made fun of her Polish and chastised her so much that she tried to erase the language and heritage from her memory. I couldn't fathom how a woman who grew up in a Polish household with parents who spoke nothing but Polish till the day they died, could not know the language. She had to speak it at home until 19 years old when she married my father. This sort of illogical behavior is what I encountered my entire life. Her Zosa family was full of similar stories you would have trouble believing. Yet that's what we had.

You could run in circles and come back to ask a question seventeen different ways, but you would always finish the conversation in the same way — empty. For those readers who have experienced living with a first generation family of that era, you know what I mean. These families faced such hardships and endured such prejudice as they grew up in the first years of the 20th century, it was not unusual for them to find that it was easier to denounce and forget their culture rather than fight to preserve it.

There were other little pearls of information that came from members on the Delphi Forum dealing with questions and issues of Poland. One contributor under "Ports of Entry" with the screen name, "Delphine2" gave a summary of her family's exodus which very closely resembled my family's story.

"In 1905, the Hamburg-American Line sailed from Hamburg to New York, the Mediterranean to New York, and Rotterdam to New York. You can find information on these sailings in a book titled, 'Morton Allan Directory' which can be found at most genealogical libraries, the National Archives or the LDS FHL (Latter Day Saints Family History Library). Poland had no port at that time, therefore it was necessary for them to travel to such far-away places as Bremen, Hamburg, Rotterdam, Antwerp and even to England. They traveled by wagons and carts to a train which took them to the port of departure.

If you find the passenger list for your ancestors you will learn to what city they traveled to the U.S. (N.Y.). I learned from his passenger list that he did not come directly to Chicago, as the family thought, but went to Brooklyn to meet with a cousin. He worked in the mills for more than 3 years before he could send for his family who arrived the week before Christmas. His wife (my grandmother) was a young woman, spoke no English and was traveling with a 6 and 4 year old to Chicago. I agree, they had guts!"

This inspired me to look into Hamburg as a potential port of entry for my grandmother Mary and Uncle Peter, since I had no success finding their records on this side of the Atlantic. I found Hamburg Link to Your Roots, written in German and English. Hamburg did a great job on this site and with their many lists. They stress "the pogroms being committed in Eastern Europe since 1881, the more than a million Jewish refugees and the other 3 million emigrants who undertook the arduous journey to Hamburg between the years of 1890 and 1914. Hamburg became the most important gateway for emigration from Eastern Europe." They knew the "Hamburg Emigration lists are ever so important, especially for Jewish organizations in the USA."

Delphi Forum Message Board members continuously mentioned Naturalization Records, Alien Registration Forms, Census lists and Austrian Army Records. My head was swimming with possibilities and places to search.

Breakthrough

I'm not sure how many letters and telephone calls I exchanged with the volunteers at the National Archives. Each time I wrote asking for information, it took weeks or more likely months, to receive a reply. I would be told that they found no record of an arrival of passengers with my family names, but the records could be in another regional archive. I was passed around from region to region sometimes two or three times as each round promised to search and cautioned me that it could take some time, but they would respond. They eventually did respond, but only to say they could not locate information about Martin or Mary. Eventually I became convinced that I might have more success searching the Boston archives in person.

I awoke in the midst of my decision to visit the National Archives in Woburn, Mass. This would be a day when no one would notice my absence. The sun was bright that early morning. A one hour drive brought me to the regional center which is a depository of many records concerning the people and affairs of the northeast.

Entering this foreign turf, I was at once lost in a sea of file cabinets and various archival records being examined by a host of researchers like myself — except that they all seemed to know much more about what they were doing than I did.

My first attempt was reviewing microfilm of the 1920 census for Fall River, where my family lived when they first came to the U.S. Although I tried several spellings of the name, my effort was fruitless. Next a clerk directed me to the microfilm containing a City Directory for Fall River from 1910 – 1914, and again there were no results. It was as if the family never existed, as my mother always said.

A very helpful clerk perceived my dilemma and offered help. It made a big difference for me to speak to someone in person. I could explain the entire story so that a detail might lead them to a worthwhile record. He suggested we try Naturalization Records even though I doubted my grandparents had been naturalized. There in a little 3 x 5 index card file, the clerk discovered my first trace of evidence which would begin to open the box of secrets. That glimmer of hope gave me the encouragement I needed to continue my search. It was a record which indicated that Peter Zosa, my uncle, had launched a search himself in 1936 or 1937. Peter had been born in Poland and traveled here with my grandmother following my grandfather's immigration several years earlier. There were actually two cards there recording his name as Peter Zosa and Peter Martin Zosa. My grandfather was Martin. I do not know why there were two cards and names. I wondered if it was an error made by a clerk who searched for both father and son and got confused.

I was taken to another small room where I completed more forms in order to have the clerk pull the original Declaration of Intent and Naturalization papers. This led me to find further documentation which incrementally took me closer to my goal, although through a maze of detours and contradictions. At each juncture, I hoped to verify names, birth places, and dates. The next piece of evidence was both helpful and confusing. It was Peter's Declaration of Intention which he had signed in August of 1937. Here was a photo of Peter with his signature 'PIOTER RZĄSA'. However, the actual document signature was Peter Zosa. This was verification of the change of name within the United States. Going from the Polish to American spelling of Peter and I assumed the same for the last name. On this Declaration, Peter gave his nationality as Polish, born in COLBRESOWA, POLAND on September 2, 1905. It states that he emigrated from Antwerp, Belgium on the Zeeland, arriving February 18, 1908. The dates agreed with everything I had heard and seen so far, but this city of birth was confusing. It was a piece of information Peter must have gleaned from his parents but was not included in my father's notes.

I presume Peter's search for dependable records continued for another couple of years until he finally completed a Petition for Naturalization form in March of 1940 – three years after his Intention. On this form, the dates of birth and arrival to the U.S. are the same, as is the port of departure, NY arrival, and name of the vessel, Zeeland. However, he answers the questions of last foreign residence and place of birth as ZAREMKACK, POLAND. Where did that come from? Now I had a collection of towns to choose from and wondered what information was correct.

The Declaration was an original document with a photo. I had copies made and submitted another form to obtain a copy of the ship's record. This was a major breakthrough for my research, as these papers established the Polish version of the name, date of arrival, the ship, and options for which town in Poland they had lived. I would return to my contact in Warsaw hoping to sort out the location of the towns and determine their proper spelling.

It must have been the new Social Security laws that inspired Peter to begin the process, since to qualify for a Social Security number and benefits, he would have to prove his citizenship. In order to gain citizenship he would have to produce information about his birth and his arrival in the United States. This put him in the very same situation as I. He contacted the National Archives to search for Arrival Information. Volunteers searched repeatedly to find a roster showing that Martin, Mary and Peter had arrived in the United States when they said they did. No records were found. The US Department of Labor Immigration and Naturalization Service determined that whereas the family had already been in the US for more than 30 years, they would issue Peter his paperwork for the purpose of naturalization on June 18, 1937, and his Oath of Allegiance on June 24, 1940. The document he signed with his Oath of Allegiance was mailed to me later with a note at the top which read:

"Certificate of Registry"

When the INS (Immigration and Naturalization Service) staff could not find a person on the manifest the applicant completed a certificate of registry form. The person had to account for all his or her time since arriving in the United States. Information can include all the places where they lived, with whom they lived, their mother's maiden name.

These papers firmly established the Polish version of my family's name. The clerk shared my delight to think that it was Peter who, in his death, had helped me. (I had shared the story of Uncle Pete who had refused to answer the door to me.) Ah, sweet retaliation!

At the end of this stream of information, I was pleased to have some consistency about Peter's birth and arrival into the United States. I felt fairly certain the date of arrival and name of the ship must be accurate, having been repeated identically so many times. However a genealogist will tell you that until you verify every detail and cross reference to other sources, one cannot be positive the information is accurate. And so, after all of this searching and waiting, I was still left without absolute verifiable information about my grandparents or their home town in Poland. Would I ever get across the ocean to some documentation showing their actual home town?

I drove to my daughter Susan's office which was just north of the National Archives. We reviewed my discovery — she shared my joy. But I think my mother was most thunderstruck when I brought my information home. She read every detail of the pages and we sat at my computer locating information on Ellis

Island and the ship, SS Zeeland, which had brought her mother and brother here.

My head was swimming with all the possibilities suggested to me about how to get to the bottom of my questions. You can spend a tiny pocket of time on the project in between other responsibilities of life, and then you are slowed by the wait for government offices to respond. Often discouraged and at a dead end, I stacked the pile of papers on a shelf for months before gathering my hopes and energy to try one more avenue of exploration.

I spoke to my mother about the many emails exchanged among my Aunt Agnes' son, my Cousin Joey's ex-wife and me. Family stories intrigued my mother – she was fascinated by the connections made with family members and the computer's ability to provide that connection. She listened and commented; sometimes she reverted back to her feelings of sadness or disgust. She said "You shouldn't talk about them when they're gone. It's in the past. It's all over. Forget about it."

This search for family roots has been compelling. Everyone brings stories of the past which have been hiding in the recesses of their emotional memory. Maybe bringing them back into the light once more and putting perspective and distance on them helps to purge the pain, heals the wounds and forgives the insensitivities. We travel an interesting path through this life.

There is a Social Security Death Index which can be accessed through the Internet. Because of the National Privacy & Disclosure Act, there is public access to information about any deceased person in the United States who became a member of Social Security. My grandparents never became citizens, nor did they ever receive any Social Security benefits. They arrived and worked in the US prior to the establishment of the Social Security Administration in 1935. The United States did not even begin tracking aliens until 1940, so while it was easy for my grandparents to be in this country without language or citizenship, no Social Security benefits were available as they aged and there was no help for this investigator tracing old records.

After Uncle Peter's death in 1992, his information became available in the Index. Instructions are given for requesting a copy of the original application to Social Security by sending a check for a small fee and some vital information to the Social Security Administration in Baltimore, Maryland.

It's a slow process. I waited months for the reply which arrived in December of 1999. The original document includes the applicant's name, address, the date and place of birth, place of employment at time of application, father's name and mother's maiden name.

This can be a treasure trove of information to anyone needing these basic clues for further investigation. In the case of

Peter, the document repeated his birth date as September 2, 1905, place of birth, Poland. Unfortunately no town in Poland was listed. It gave parents' names as Martin Zosa and Mary Wieluba, which was the information I had from my father's notes. No big news, but another verification of his birth date and I thought the name "Wieluba" was pretty certain.

And then there was Nikifory

As 1999 was coming to an end, I was feeling more and more eager to find answers to my many questions. The Polish Forum members suggested I write to the archdiocese of Rzeszow, Poland, which might contain the records of all the small towns in the region I was studying. That would be the likely repository for the south-east corner or province. They likened the city to our "American Buffalo city." Someone supplied the address for the archdiocese of Rzeszow but cautioned that I must write in Polish.

I prepared a letter asking for the vital records of Marcin, Maryanna and Peter with approximate dates for their births, marriage and emigration. I put out a call on the message boards for translation. There was Nikifory once again. What a wonderful Christmas present it was to establish a relationship as we switched over to our private email addresses and started a more personal dialogue.

I learned that Nikifory was a 35 year old Polish woman

named Gosia living in Warsaw, with a linguistics background, completing her MA in Semantics. Her university study had broadened to include the history and origin of the English language and English and American literature as well. One of her passions was the history of language and word formation. Small wonder she was drawn to the Forums many discussions of names, towns, and origins. She explained she had recently purchased a "Names and Surnames" set of dictionaries and had culled several pieces of information from them.

1. Re: the spelling of my mother's first name, Amelia was most likely.
2. Grandmother's maiden name of WIELUBA may be correct but there was no one with that name alive in Poland as of 1990.
3. There were over 10,000 persons with the name of Skowron, none with Skowrok or Skalron as it had been misspelled in family notes.
4. She found more than 500 persons with the surname of Czeczot.
5. Finally she found that as of 1990 there were only 1687 persons with the name Rząsa.

Also among my Christmas gifts was the complete translation of my letter to the archdiocese along with the recommendation to start the letter with "Praise the Lord Jesus Christ" as opposed to my rather bland "Greetings." Gosia changed my Maryanne to the more likely equivalent Marianna and Peter became Piotr.

She suggested I offer to send a donation as opposed to including it. She concluded with "Meanwhile, have a very Merry Christmas and a smashingly Happy New Year."

I couldn't believe I was so lucky as to find this amazing resource and pen pal. And I rejoiced!

The Church of Latter Day Saints has had the reputation of holding the greatest repository of family information of any church or organization in the world. Their mission includes sending missionaries throughout the world to gather data about families and convey it back to the central archives in Salt Lake City, Utah. I was in a local store one day in February, 2000, when I fell into a conversation with someone who told me that although the archives were in Utah, there was a way to access the records through various local churches. The regional center was in a church on Narragansett Parkway not more than a mile from my home. I planned a visit to learn more about their services. Entering the rear corner of the building, I discovered there were a series of small rooms dedicated to researching family records. Volunteers worked three days a week overseeing resources. I found a volunteer who pointed out what was available through a series of volumes packed into a tiny room along with index cards and a computer terminal connected to a mainframe computer in Utah. It would allow us to access the information at the center in Utah and order specific rolls of microfilm which they would send to this local branch. A second room held a number of microfilm viewing machines lining all four walls. Still another room held a variety of equipment which allowed access to several kinds of tapes and chronicles. Volunteers were busy moving amongst these rooms to answer questions, assist with technical equipment or discuss alternatives for researching your family. Here is where I learned about the Soundex System.

The call came from a volunteer at the local chapter of "Latter Day Saints" telling me my microfilm had arrived. I altered my schedule to allow myself a couple of hours in the Center, and packed up my case of notes, binders and pens. I had ordered three rolls of microfilm which the volunteer helped me load into the viewing machine. I remember thinking how archaic these viewers seemed, hardly changing in the 20 or so years since I had last used one. The images sometimes blurred or were wider than the screen. The handwritten entries varied with the skill of the writer. I was looking at actual ships' manifests with dates of arrival, ship's names, and countries of origin. This was authentic. Here is where all my answers should be found. The hours disappeared and the volunteers at the center gave the warning call to close down and prepare to leave. I would have to return for another session of tedious, eye crossing work on another day. I had developed a method to deal with all this information, however. Knowing I would unlikely go through this exercise again, I had undertaken to record on paper all the names which might be related to the family. Having been told my grandfather left numerous brothers behind in Poland, I couldn't take the chance that some of those entries were uncles, cousins, or descendants of his brothers. At some point I might connect the dots – complete a full account of the movement of the Zosa clan from Poland to points all over the United States.

The ports of departure varied as well as ship names, but the Port of NY was consistently listed as the arrival point. It took some time for me to accept that. I was so certain they would have sailed into Fall River. I am still in awe of the transportation nightmare of getting first from Poland to Belgium or England and later from NYC to Fall River, Massachusetts visualizing them in 1906, without reading skills and very little money, my respect grows as I envision the courage it must have taken to complete the migration over land in addition to the arduous ocean voyage.

My hope of completing this microfilm exploration was unrealistic. I had to return to the Center several times for a few hours at each visit. Rolling down the manifest with hundreds of names, excitedly I stopped at every Zosa, Rząsa, or similar name. Tediously I recorded each of their arrivals until my pages filled with dozens of entries. Surely some of these passengers were part of my family.

These sessions continued as I ordered more microfilm to be sent from Utah – and until I felt I had gleaned every ounce of information available through this source. Using notes from my father and minimal clues from Peter's records, I referenced the book of ship arrivals, ports of entry, ports of departure. If I could only gather all this data into a room where I would sit for days unraveling the connections between me and these brave travelers from another time...another world.

In an effort to manage all this information, I later entered all the names and passport information into my computer so I could have more readable lists to work with. In our imperfect world, my computer later needed to be replaced, viruses attacked, system crashed, and all other possible computer disasters taught me hard lessons about data collection. All the voices of experience instructing me to back up my information on a disc echoed in my head. Some of these research excursions will never be repeated but the information gathered could become more meaningful over time. My lessons learned have been to not throw away the sloppy pages of initial collection material; print as soon as entries are computerized; and to definitely save on discs, zip drive, or whatever device is available. Another unfortunate circumstance for me has been that my search has spanned so many years, different computer systems and computer programs – that my records sometimes don't translate forward to the newest versions in technology. We've all complained about how obsolete our equipment and programs become within a brief time. It forces us to trade up, improve, become faster, all of which is dandy, but often at the expense of losing documents which may not "translate" to the higher level. The 5" floppy shifted to 3½" discs, the Zip drive gave way to rewriteable CD and Microsoft Word programs changed so many features that old documents would later be gibberish when you tried to advance to the newer system and "improved" program.

My friends were pulled into my search as well as anyone I met along the way who had the slightest interest in Poland or genealogy. I have close friends who were living in Manhattan during this time. Sam is an Anthropologist with Cornell University introducing students to a variety of ethnic pockets in the city as well as museums, cultural organizations and the immigrant experience at Ellis Island. I decided to tag along with Sam and his students the day they visited Ellis Island. The boat ride was sunny and breezy, the students chattered happily, but my mind was filled with visions of ships arriving with hundreds of passengers who were thankful to have survived the long voyage.

I left them at the boat. I was glad to be alone as I walked into the huge building which had served as the intake center for thousands of immigrants entering the United States. Being alone allowed me to envision what it must have been like for those foreign borns. In particular I tried to imagine my grandmother coming with a small child. Enlarged posters on the walls show the actual groups arriving...often women with small children and only a small basket or suitcase filled with personal belongings. There were pictures of the endless lines of rumpled, tired travelers worn from their journey. Their eyes looked dazed as they were processed through this cavernous hall – their minds filled with anxiety, fear, hope and determination.

A favorite display was a platform about 30 feet long piled high with suitcases, carpet bags, sacks and satchels of all description. The age, origin and wear on these bags told a story in themselves.

Guided tours explained the procedure used to process the thousands of arrivals coming like waves – boat load after boat load. It was the story of the biggest immigration of people at any time in the history of the world. The peak year was 1907 when 1,004,747 immigrants were received here. The all-time high was on April 17 of that year when a total of 11,747 immigrants were processed, all in one day.

They climbed the stairs to the Great Hall, with doctors watching them to see if anyone was limping or having trouble breathing on the stairs. Ill health could be a reason for detention or deportation. I learned that ship owners carried these people as cargo to offset their costs of the trip to Canada.

They were primarily interested in crossing the Atlantic to pick up lumber from Canada and deliver it to Europe. Carrying passengers one way made the round trip a very profitable venture for the ship owners. Their agreement with the American government was that they would carry only passengers with proper documentation, in good health, with a prescribed number of dollars and a sponsor to care for them once they landed in the U.S. There was to be no burden created for the United States. If a passenger didn't meet the criteria, they would be returned to the port from which they came, at the ship owner's expense. When I heard that, my mind went back to the conversation I had with my mother and Aunt Agnes. They repeated a story which had been floating in the family for years. It was suspected that my grandmother and uncle Peter had arrived as stow-a ways on a boat. That was their reasoning when paperwork couldn't be located to document their trip. I realized how impossible that would have been in the situation I saw here at Ellis Island. There would be no way for a woman and small child to slip through all of those check points without being discovered and deported. No, these imagined explanations for what they didn't know or understand was the result of first generation Americans having insufficient knowledge of the way government operated. My mother and her siblings probably never grasped the magnitude of the event their parents were a part of. Now that I have made the crossing to that distant land, experienced the contrast between the two nations, and walked the Great Hall of Ellis Island, I am in awe of these people. They had such courage. Their strong will, bravery, and spirit are astounding to me. Could I abandon my homeland, family, friends and all that is familiar to take the chance that I would survive the passage and find a better way in some strange place I knew little about?

There were exhibits to walk through giving you that same feeling of being processed. A series of small rooms showed where they could buy box lunches and exchange currency. There was the feared detention bunk room, the "kissing room" where you joined your sponsor, the hospital where you had an opportunity to proceed or be deported. Another favorite display included personal items brought by immigrants which have now been donated to the museum. It was fascinating to see what was considered precious when only a couple of pieces of luggage could be brought into the new country. There was a small concertina from Poland on display. I photographed it for Nana. I imagined it to be like the one her father had.

Signs directed you to the trains headed for Chicago and Pennsylvania. I questioned the research which said my Uncle Pete gave NYC as their arrival city aboard the U.S.S. Zeeland. Most people coming to Ellis Island boarded trains going west – seldom is New England mentioned. My inclination was to begin the search again in Massachusetts to see if they actually came into Fall River or Boston as I originally presumed.

I had lunch on the sunny patio and lined up for the ferry with people of many nationalities and cultures. We filed onto the boat, sat on rows of benches (like the Great Hall) and passed the Statue of Liberty – as they had.

Losing Nana 2001

My mother taught me something every day in quiet ways and by example. They were simple lessons about nature, patience, appreciation, about being thankful, humble, hardworking, strong, loyal, frugal, gracious and spiritual. Stopping in to check on her each day gave me a moment to ponder whether or not I will have such contentment at the end of my life. She

1900s · · · · · 1920s · · · · · 1960s · · · · · 1970s · · · · · 1980s · · · · · 1990s

was such a quiet yet powerful little woman. I didn't always know that. I'm glad she stayed long enough to teach me. She was such a rare and precious gift.

We all referred to her as Nana, and she was special to everyone who surrounded her. I doubt I could master her art of touching each person's soul without a lot of words or fuss. She survived my father for 22 years, living independently and providing each of us with a touchstone that grounded us.

By the time her 89th birthday came, her body was tired and it took daily visits by my husband, daughter and me to help her continue her life in the home she loved up to her last day. She left us February 25, 2001. Her wake was filled with an outpouring of love, respect, and admiration so many people had for this modest soul. As usual, family members seldom seen otherwise were there, and the stories told were so "family" – so "Zosa."

Uncle Michael was now the last of the Zosa siblings alive. He and Aunt Jennie came to each session of the wake and funeral. They amused us with their banter. I've learned to love these "wake stories." Sometimes I wish I had a tape recorder for all the family information and folk lore that emerges during these events.

One of their stories was about how they met and married. Mike and Jenny worked in a factory together – now Union Paper in Providence. As Jenny was walking to another area to get supplies, a co-worker stopped her. She handed Jenny a Baby Ruth candy bar. She said, "You see that guy over there?" Jenny

2001 · · · ·

looked toward Michael. "He says you're his girlfriend and he's gonna marry you." The co-worker told her. I asked Michael why he did that and he glibly answered something about her looking good and him wanting to have a wife – then he added that he wanted to get out of the house to get away from Peter, his older brother! Jenny adds, regarding the Baby Ruth, "He didn't even pay for it! He was so cheap!" "We used slugs from the shop to put in the candy machine." She went on to talk about their first and only date. She said, "Wherever we were, he bought some popcorn and ate the whole thing himself. Then near the end of the box, he asked if I wanted some, but just the bad un-popped kernels were left by then." All of their stories are sprinkled with laughter by everyone around – as well as the two of them. "And yet you married him anyway," I noted. "Yes." They married and he left for 3½ years in the Army, traveling to Europe, and on to Austria. They joked, too, about her wanting the allotment check and his life insurance policy. Their banter is so good natured that even when they say they were fighting or arguing about driving directions in the car, you have to think that they must get over their arguments pretty fast.

Michael also shared his memory of my mother's wedding. He recalled there was a three piece "orchestra" and he chuckled. It was a bass, a violin, and an accordion. The food was downstairs at the house on Derry Street and the dancing was upstairs. He said people were putting money in the hole of the bass – and he watched with fascination. He was only about 12 years old. Jenny chimes in that he was hanging around to see if any money fell on the floor that he could get for himself! They laugh again. He doesn't deny the accusation. He had forgotten who my father's best man was and I told him it was my Uncle Bill, (my father's brother) or Wilfred as they would have known him. I reminded him that one of the Czeczot daughters was the maid of honor and Nana had borrowed the wedding veil from the other Czeczot sister. (The Czeczot family sprang from my grand-father's step-sister, Agnes Skowron Czeczot.)

There were messages left in a guest book at the entrance to the room of the wake — tender thoughts and memories of Amelia. My daughter wrote a treasured remembrance that describes the kind of relationship my mother had with her. Such a contrast to what Nana experienced with her mother, and she never knew any grandparents.

2001 • • • •

Wedding of Amelia Zosa and Hervé Hudon

In Thinking About Nana...

'A family ought to have an identity that gives each member a sense of belonging.'

For me, that is my Nana. She was someone who brightened my day, gave me a chuckle, and kept me whole when I was unravelly, and instinctively fed me soup when I needed it most. She was a woman who perfected the art of grand mothering and did so with modesty and ease. There were several things I did for Nana on a regular basis and she was so extremely appreciative and always tried to find ways to pay me back. I had to remind her that I would do any one of these things for a million years just because it was for her.

Having my grandmother in my life to my late 30s is extraordinary and unique. My relationship with her has carved my personality, my values, and my definition of self and family. In the coming years her influence will reveal itself in the ways I will lead my life. She was certainly a woman of quiet strength, thoughtfulness, personal grace and an independent spirit. She pursued her desires in a subtle but intentional way and in doing so; put her life together in the way she meant to live it. Surrounded by the people who meant the most to her, the memories that she wished to keep, and the comfort of a home she loved.

She was a friend to me. She gathered me. When my pieces scattered, she gathered and gave them back to me in all the right order and made my world right again.

Her pride and joy in my life has made me feel successful. She lavished in my achievements and was angry with me in my disappointments, travelling in my business suit and exploring the world she so admired. It gives me confidence and pride and I am never alone in my endeavors.

To say that I will miss her company and cups of tea is an

2001   · · · ·

understatement. Her presence will always be felt, and she will continue to complete the mystical triad that exists with my mother and me.

XO Susan

One of Amelia's good friends from her Senior Citizen Club wrote in the guest book:

And so our mothers and grandmothers have, more often than not anonymously, handed on the creative spark, the seed of the flower they themselves never hoped to see, or like a sealed letter they could not plainly read.

– Alice Walker

My mother had inspired my search for my grandfather's roots. I wanted to put the pieces of his life together for her to know and appreciate. She adored her father. I had hoped my research would uncover ways for her to develop pride in her heritage, get past the shame she had felt in childhood.

Mourning turned into determination as I gathered the energy to combine an aggressive search with my daily work and family life. My focus on grandfather's village intensified.

Unconfirmed

In April of 2001, for the first time online, the Ellis Island Immigration Records became available to the public. Seventeen million immigrants sailed into NY harbor between the years of 1892-1924 and now the manifests of the ships could be accessed from anywhere throughout the world, so long as they had one of those magical instruments of technology – the computer with Internet access. The officials at the Statue of Liberty-Ellis Island Foundation expected millions to use the newly created site. But, in fact, so many people tried to access these records in the first days they actually swamped the site causing technical difficulties and forced a shutdown in order to increase the site's capabilities for heavier traffic. The problems were tended to swiftly and access to the site resumed promptly.

The Mormon Church provided the labor to put the information together for the new site. According to a newspaper account, it took about 12,000 volunteer members about eight years to extract the data from microfilms. They dealt with 22 million passenger records and 60-year-old microfilm. The original passenger manifests weren't available for inspection when clarity or spelling was in question. The government sold those original documents for paper pulp years earlier. If ship personnel wrote names of families or towns phonetically because of language problems, it could complicate the investigation. However there are tips offered for alternative spellings, which might give the needed clue to finding a relative. When a match

2001 · · · ·

is found, the seeker would be given the name of the ship their relative sailed on, the departure and arrival dates, the name of the relative's contact in the United States, and the name of anyone sailing with the relative. There are also entries giving age, last place of residence, marital status, and brief physical description. All of this would have taken researcher weeks of work and travel to the location housing these microfilms, but now you could sit at your home computer station, click your mouse and find your family. In this site, you can sort and edit your search profile instantly. A search can be made by name, year of arrival, ethnicity, port of departure, name of ship and several other options. For today's computer programmers these are simple, basic tasks in many of the programs they write. To the descendant of an Eastern European whose family has been lost to them for decades, these possibilities seem positively miraculous. The site is located at www.ellisislandrecords.org. In addition there is a Family History Gift Shop with items for sale that relate to family history or to Ellis Island. Finally, you can become a member of The Statue of Liberty-Ellis Island Foundation for $45 a year. Membership includes the option to create and maintain Your Family History Scrapbook, get discounts, and importantly, to help support the work of this important foundation.

A donation can be sent to have a family name added to the Wall of Honor. It's a lasting memorial to one's ancestors. I proudly entered MARCIN RZĄSA AND FAMILY.

I applaud Lee Iacocca for spearheading the Ellis Island

restoration project and urge everyone to visit their website as well as this glorious achievement in New York harbor.

My frustration was building with each letter I received from the National Archives and each failed attempt to discover that one simple piece of information...where had my grandparents come from when they came to the States in the early 1900s? Each clue I uncovered indicated a different town or there was no record found. This last series of letters was leading me to believe that the only solution was for me to go to Washington, D.C. and search the main source of the data. My annual birthday trip to D.C. was the opportunity I needed. I went alone that year and stayed in a wonderful Bed & Breakfast just behind the Capitol. Springtime in D.C. is magnificent with magnolias, tulips, cherry blossoms, and sunshine. In preparation for the trip, I emailed the National Archives for some direction so I would save time in the city. I explained that I had found the package of information about my Uncle Peter, and the volunteer I spoke to on the phone had suggested I "search other ships' arrivals using one year earlier/later, etc." My email was returned on the same day with the following message.

"Dear Ms. Hartman, The records you want will be at the National Archives (700 Pennsylvania Avenue, NW, Washington, DC) Most of the indices to the various ports of arrival cover a span of years, so with any luck you will find the records. Aside from trying different dates, you might want to consider trying various spelling of the name. Good luck!"

I walked the wide avenues to the National Archives, went

2001 · · · ·

through their security check and found my way to the floor where miles of microfilm are stored. There are volunteers along the way to help you become acquainted with their resources. A huge room is filled with rows of microfilm viewing machines. A bank of drawers on the wall gives you coded numbers for the actual films. You walk into the next room, which is like a huge vault, and find the shelf where your particular film is stored. It's amazing that so many pieces of information and numerous rolls of film can be kept in order and accessible to the general public, moving things in and out all day, every day. Dozens of seekers wind through reel after reel as the machines grind away through the hours. I took my place among them following the directions I was given, and fell into the rhythm of the room.

There was no entry for Martin Zosa or for Marcin Rząsa. I returned to the volunteer desk. With new directions, I retraced my steps being careful to choose the correct film and wind through another mile or so of tape. Martin was not on the indicated page. Three or four times I repeated my questions to volunteers and the process with the reels, but with no success. I knew the information had to be here somewhere. All suggestions from volunteers failed. My resolve strengthened. I wouldn't leave without my treasure, no matter how maddening I might be to these busy volunteers. If I was at fault in the way I searched I would continue to ask questions and repeat the process until I got it right. About the fifth time I returned to the volunteer station, a young man decided he would undertake the mission with me — walking me through the steps. I

1900s · · · · · 1920s · · · · · 1960s · · · · · 1970s · · · · · 1980s · · · · · 1990s

watched closely as he located the indices and film and proceeded to wind. The name was not on the page where the index said it would be. Where I had given up at that point, he continued on. His experience with finding errors in the system made him confident. He knew by this time that I wasn't likely to leave the building without some information and perhaps he had the same vision of me refusing to leave at the end of the day. I'm smiling now, but that is the way I felt at the moment – so far along this endless search and so exasperated with these records. Screen after screen of eye straining lists revolved through the viewer, with this young man's trained scrutiny persevering. Suddenly he stopped the film at the top of a page totally unrelated to the page number we were directed to. There at the top of the list was Rząsa, Marcin, age 25, laborer, arrived Oct. 6, 1906, into the Port of New York through Liverpool on the S.S. Carmania. Place of birth given as Pajecryna in Austria. I could have hugged that man and shouted through all the corridors of the building, I was so excited.

There was finally a valid record for me to work with. That precious link from the U.S. to his homeland was made. This connection would get me back to a town where more information would be stored. I would know where to look and have some dates to help narrow the search. It's hard to describe the joy of finally finding something tangible to document this simple man's courageous journey. Years of his family feeling a subtle insignificance without records to show or documents to legitimize were now gradually morphing into a family history. We

2001 . . . .

were on our way to piecing his story together, knowing where we all came from and what soil bore the first roots of our family. What a find! The sunshine on the big Mall outside the Capitol and the Smithsonian Institute's magnificent collection of buildings couldn't have been more brilliant than my absolute elation.

I made copies of each section of the manifest where grandfather's information was listed, even though the film and copies were fuzzy and barely readable. It gave me something to refer to over and over again. What initially seems like very brief facts can actually develop into considerably more of the story.

Returning to the Internet, photographs of the ship and its history can be found through a site named Kinships.com. Full sized reproduction posters can be purchased. There are photos of the ships at dock in Liverpool, which gives a sense of that part of the journey. Liverpool was an enormous port teeming with immigrant passengers bound for their new world. I could imagine the chaos of such a place as these people who had never traveled beyond their simple village were now thrown into a bedlam of activity and foreign languages.

The manifest also offers information about the address where each passenger intends to go when they reach the U.S. Sponsors, money to care for one's self, an address, transportation from N.Y. to their eventual destination, all have to be accounted for as they enter the Ellis Island intake center. In the case of my grandfather, the name given for a sponsor was a "brother-in-law," but the actual name is not legible. The address was 63 Milton Street, but no city or state was listed. I would have to presume that Milton Street was in Fall River where I know they went to live and where my mother was born. The "Brother-in-law" could be inaccurate as we have no family stories or documentation that would indicate a sister in this country. There has only been the story of my grandfather being sponsored by his "step sister." The mysterious "brother-in-law" story would have to unfold over time.

In my haste and frequent frustration during this long search, I've never taken time to thank all the endless clerks and volunteers at the assorted offices of the National Archives and regional offices of the Dept. of Labor Immigration and Naturalization Service. Numerous times they made the extra effort to call me long distance to report progress or lack thereof – and often gave me suggestions for alternatives to explore. They must realize how significant these searches can be. Their sensitivity and persistence is so meaningful to someone immersed in the struggle to find their heritage.

I did take some time to thank my crazy Uncle Peter. Here was my first real breakthrough in finding evidence of my history – and the information was supplied through Peter's documentation giving me the correct family name. That strange and uncooperative uncle, who wouldn't answer the door to me, was helping me to make the leap from the United States to Poland. How strange, poetic and wonderful these little moments are, along the way of the seeker.

2001 · · · ·

While I was at the National Archives I took the opportunity to check their 1920 Census Records. I was still curious about the family's early years in this country. I wanted to visit each address where they had lived and compare the data of the census records with the information I had already collected. All the experienced researchers and genealogists I ever spoke with cautioned me to continually search for verification because of inaccuracies that occur in many documents as well as in the memory of family members.

Sadly I found Amelia Zosa, my mother, listed in the 1920 census as an "inmate" at the State Home at the age of six. The word "inmate" on the page still stops me cold. I try to imagine that kind of childhood and want it to be a mistake. There was no other family name listed at the state home in that census. My mother referred to "we" when she told me about being placed there. Was it a mistake of the census taker or was she the only child sent there? Maybe Peter was allowed to stay home because he was thirteen years old at the time, but Agnes would have been only two years old.

I was reminded of my mother's childhood again when I returned from D.C. The following Sunday, *Providence Journal* ran a story about the State Home and the children. There was a man at the Department of Children Youth and Families (DCYF) who was researching their old records for the Trinity

Square Repertory Company. They were planning to do a play about those unfortunate children titled, "Cider House Rules." It was discovered that Rhode Island had one of the first public orphanages in the country. I had intentions of contacting the DCYF worker for more information but I had too many avenues to explore and not enough hours in my days to look into every aspect of my mother's life and family.

I continued to wonder if she was institutionalized more than once. It must have made quite an impression on her. She felt such shame for herself and her parents – part of the reason she never wanted to help me with memories or research. There were too many dark crevices in her formative years.

The weeks following my discovery at the National Archives were filled with thoughts of Poland. I was now in steady contact with Gosia, who was the "voice" on the other end of the Polish forum. We had progressed to writing to one another on our personal emails and were beginning to feel more familiar.

Another young woman, Joanna (from the Polish Forum) in Kraków had committed to my search as well. Both of them were trying to find any trace of information about the family name or any of the towns mentioned in the various documents I had already gathered.

Once again I must mention how impressed I have always been with the Polish peoples' willingness to be helpful. They go to far greater lengths than I have experienced anywhere else.

Excerpts from our emails give an idea of how much effort was being put into my search and the sources we examined. I

2001 · · · ·

had come to the conclusion I would have to complete the search in person traveling to Poland and using a translator to guide me through the hinterlands of southern Poland. Joanna and Gosia volunteered to translate during parts of the trip as well as doing some advance work to locate the town mentioned in the National Archives microfilm. They simultaneously searched for our family name in phone books or census records.

From Joanna in April, "I've checked phone directories for Rzeszów and Kolbuszowa (Gosia had found the correct spelling on one of her maps). There are no people called Wieluba, (grandmother's maiden name) but there are over thirty names 'Rząsa' in Rzeszów, some more in Kolbuszowa and surrounding villages. I think there may be more people named Rząsa in any of the towns – who simply don't have a telephone (if you can imagine this). These names seem pretty popular in this region. I'll try to get hold of the directory for Częstochowa. Perhaps it will be easier to start looking for the name Wieluba. I'll try to find out when the first census was carried out in this century – and how to get to this information. If we need maps or some archive information from the 'Austrian' period we contact Vienna or Lwow. It is possible that the information will be accessible there. The good news is the Austrians had very good archives (as you probably know)."

Later Joanna reported, "I've started asking people about documents and censuses and I've found out there may be a lot of information in parishes but also in courts' records. After 1918 when Poland re-gained independence there were more regular censuses and they were carried out in a pretty organized way. Thanks to Poland's twisted history they had to list the citizens quite often to find out whose left."

I thought that information would be helpful to others trying to find connections and family during later years, but of course my grandfather had already left Poland by 1918, so census records were not likely to be helpful. We moved on to trying to find the hometown mentioned in the ship's records. By May we were still wondering if we were ever going to find this place. "I've been trying to locate Pajeczyna, Pajecyrna and unfortunately, with no success. No such place was in Galicia in 1880 or in "Krolestwo" i.e. the Russian-occupied territory (to which Viktoria and Częstochowa belonged). I've checked the lists of towns and villages made on the basis of the 1880 census. They are very detailed – comprise all places, even the smallest. Next thing was the list of villages and towns in Austro-Hungary published 1905 (no Pajecyrna etc.) as well. Then there was a big census in 1921 after we regained independence. There is no such place in the new 'Poland'. In the provinces of Lwow and Stanislawow, which belong to Ukraine now, also – nothing. I've discussed the matter with people who work at the archives of the library (Jagiellonian University) and they say we could compare Austrian maps from 1870s and the ones made later to check if Payecyrna could have changed its name. But to do this we need more about location. Any place around Pajecyrna, post-office? County name? Could you send me a scan of the document you sent me before? We need something between Pajecyrna

2001 . . . .

and Austria. I could try to decipher it with the women at the library; they've got much experience with such things and are professionals, and they're willing to help. By the way, they told me that people from all continents come to look for their roots to this library."

Unfortunately the ship's records are not as complete as Joanna may have wished. There may have been more information submitted to the authorities in order to make the trip to the U.S. but only minimal information was shown on the ship's manifest...or on the microfilm. It appeared that although these resources might be valuable in another person's search for family, Joanna's efforts would prove fruitless for me.

By the first days of September, we decided that although the ship's manifest gave Pajecyrna as Marcin's home town, Gosia concluded it must have been a reference to Pajęczno which is just north of Częstochowa, and both are northwest of Kraków. We planned to search each of the towns mentioned in Marcin or Peter's documents to determine the more accurate information. We conjectured that Marcin could have been stationed in one of those towns while in the Austrian Army, which might account for the variations. Another letter came from the Immigration & Naturalization Service September 10 to report that they had searched for "records that relate to your request and determined that if such records exist, they would be maintained under the jurisdiction of the INS office at the following address"...in Lee's Summit, Missouri! They forwarded my request to the Missouri office. That written request had bounced from one office to the next for several years while I knew by now that the reason they hadn't been successful was that Marcin was listed on the wrong page of the ship's manifest. I would never have found that information if I hadn't gone in person to D.C. and badgered the volunteers until we found the entry for grandfather, pages away from where we should have found it. I also knew that my personal visit to Poland was vital. All these letters, requests, and searching records online or by Joanna and Gosia were not going to replace my trudging from town to town, parish to parish, relentlessly searching for grandfather's village and the vital records proving the family's birth and marriage dates.

2001 . . . .

Second Trip
to Poland

Warsaw

⁕

Pajęczno

⁕

Częstochowa

⁕

Kraków

⁕

Rzeszów

⁕

Kolbuszowa

In the fall of 2001, armed with a notebook full of all the significant pieces of information I had gathered about the Zosa family, Hoot, Susan and I packed off to Poland with firm resolve to find my grandfather's village. This would be a mission focused on family search with very little time devoted to tourist attractions. My husband and daughter agreed with the

------ Route Traveled 2001

agenda. They were excited about the trip, but part of their reason for coming was they were afraid for me going alone. We had all been raised to distrust the Soviet Bloc and although the Iron Curtain had fallen, we were still reading stories of black market business, remnants of the KGB, dangerous thieves, and unscrupulous taxi drivers. I was certain everything would be fine especially with my internet friend to guide me. Gosia was at the airport to meet us with a sign that read "Pawtuxet" so we would recognize each other. You couldn't miss her, being the six foot tall lady she is, and the sign was a perfect ice breaker to start us laughing and developing a familiarity instantly. We

found our way to the flat we rented on the third floor of a building only 2 blocks from the main square of Old Town, Warsaw,
which would be our base of operations while in the country. It
was a simply furnished two-bedroom rental with fully supplied
kitchen, laundry facilities and a large living room, including TV
that received CNN news in English. From there we could rent a
car to drive to the various towns mentioned in the documents I
had found during my search for our origin. We got acquainted
with Gosia and mapped out our plan for the coming days.

The first day would be spent in and around Old Town which
my daughter had never seen, and my husband and I had never
forgotten. We insisted Susan see the little museum at the corner
of the square where they show a brief film of Warsaw during
WWII with all the bombing and systematic leveling of Warsaw.
It tells the story of the tenacity of the Poles as they returned to
the City. Using old photos, paintings and memory, they sifted
through the rubble to find the pieces they would use to rebuild
the city exactly as it was before the bombs fell. Women and
children cleaned brick, broken crucifixes were reattached to
walls of churches and every detail was reconstructed painstak-
ingly. It's a very powerful story which hardly seems believable
when you stand in the cobblestone square surrounded by such
handsomely decorated early architecture.

Hoot returned to our flat for a nap while Gosia, Susan and
I explored the city further. It wasn't long before Gosia received
a text on her cell phone alerting her to a horror which had just
occurred in New York. At first she didn't believe it, but she knew

1900s · · · · · 1920s · · · · · 1960s · · · · · 1970s · · · · · 1980s · · · · · 1990s

her friend Peter wouldn't joke like that. She realized there was a very real and serious situation. We rushed to a hotel building to ask if anyone could verify the story. They had heard about it and, realizing we were Americans, immediately brought us to a private office with a TV where CNN was broadcasting the news. We watched the destruction of the twin towers in New York City by terrorists flying American planes into two enormous skyscrapers. Thunderstruck we returned to our flat to watch the chaotic news reports as events of the day rolled out from one attack to the next in New York, Washington, DC, and Pennsylvania. We thought of the people we knew in those states who might be affected and wondered what all of this would mean to the country, the future, and to our travel in the coming weeks. I began to formulate contingency plans in my head in the event we were stranded in Poland for a prolonged period of time.

Hours of CNN news rolled past our disbelieving eyes. We felt the coincidence of having just watched the film showing the bombing of Warsaw and simultaneously learning that New York had been attacked. Americans have lived under the delusion that nothing would ever touch us on American soil. Wars and bombings happened in other countries, but never in the United States. No one was prepared for such news, including the Poles and Gosia. All communications were closed by the United States, including telephone and email. Everything stopped while heads reeled and officials attempted to grasp what had just happened. We were scheduled to begin our tour the following day and we decided we would include a stop at

2001 . . . .

the American Consulate in Kraków to get more information. We didn't know if there would be flights into the States when we were scheduled to go home. Air traffic remained suspended while the government tried to sort out the horrors. It was a strange feeling to know all of what was happening at home while completely out of touch. Everything went on lock down. We could only continue with our plans for Poland and hope to learn more in the coming days.

Driving south from Warsaw, the suburbs pass and the terrain becomes more rural. The roads are smaller than we are accustomed to but with less traffic we move quickly towards Częstochowa, the first town on my list to be explored. We checked into the Hotel Scout and motored off to the town and the monastery which houses the famous Black Madonna. The main sanctuary is an absolutely stunning art piece in the Baroque style with fat cherubs and heavy gold leaf used on much of the ornamentation. The lighting was dim adding to the peaceful warm glow of the place. Thousands of devout Poles come from miles away (often on foot) to make a pilgrimage to this sacred place. Other Poles living along the route give free food and lodging to the pilgrims as they make their way to pay homage to what they believe is a miraculous painting and place.

We explored the chapels, museum, archways and courtyard of this magnificent enclave attempting to grasp the significance it holds for these devoted people. I wondered if the notes of my father's papers meant that my grandfather had come here in a pilgrimage, or was it a place he came with the Austrian Army?

1900s · · · · · 1920s · · · · · 1960s · · · · · 1970s · · · · · 1980s · · · · · 1990s

Could it be the town where he was born?

We found the library at the town center and poured over volumes of family listings. There was no trace of my family's name or any variation of the name. We were also checking telephone books along our way, but there was no trace of Zosa or Rząsa.

We returned to our hotel after dinner at a charming restaurant where the owner was thrilled to have American visitors. The hotel manager was proud to allow us to use his computer to check on various friends in the States. Everyone we knew was accounted for after the horrors of 9/11, but we remained uncertain about our return trip home. We continued to live in the moment, enjoying the adventure we were in and somehow we hoped things would settle down before it was time for our flight back to the states.

Traveling along the country roads to Pajęczno, we enjoyed the homemade shrines posted for farmers who stopped to pray when they didn't have time to get to the church. These shrines become more plentiful in this southern agricultural region. Men driving horse carts with vegetables, families working the fields, tiny markets dotting the roads, lots of poplar, birch and pine trees, all were intriguing as we moved through a land where time stood still. Their homes are simple block or brick built during the Socialist era when there would have been only a couple of choices for style – none of which should set you apart or make you look wealthy, as directed by communist rule.

The next town was Pajęczno, the closest name we could find to the Pajecyrna listed on the ship's manifest as my grandfather's

2001 · · · ·

home. I had found a contact on the internet who lived in this town and we planned to meet. He was Borek, a student who had managed to build his own computer, eager to move into the modern age. His mother worked at Town Hall where everyone was buzzing about the visiting Americans and all the records were checked for our name. There was no trace of the family. A history teacher from the high school was brought into the mix, having recently written a history of the village. He volunteered to take us to several adjoining towns and churches, calling ahead to connect with a priest who would agree to search the old books from the 1800s. These priests were sometimes climbing up on stools, sometimes on their knees digging around for volumes from the years in question. Our guide, Gosia was crucial to all this searching, translating constantly throughout the day.

People stared as we stood in the street or moved through the high school corridors, whispering amongst themselves. We were rare curiosities in this tiny off-the-beaten-path town. As people continued their chatter in Town Hall, a business man overheard the conversations and offered that he had heard my family's name in Rzeszów. It was one more lead to explore...one more town in which to check phone books and church records. We thanked these gracious people who had given up so much of their day and imagined they enjoyed our visit. No doubt we were nearly the only Americans who had ever visited this little place. We left Pajęczno touched by the warmth and openness of these people. We felt like ambassadors bringing goodwill from across the globe.

(1900s) · · · · · (1920s) · · · · · (1960s) · · · · · (1970s) · · · · · (1980s) · · · · · (1990s)

Ending the day with a good dinner and wonderful hosts at the Hotel Scout, we reorganized our thoughts with Gosia, planning another exploration in Rzeszów. We mapped our drive to Kraków first, as Gosia insisted we must see this important authentic city, which is her favorite in Poland. We had arranged lodging near the center and we were scheduled to meet another volunteer guide from my internet searches. The plan was to turn in the rental car, tour Kraków, and then move on to Rzeszów by train. Gosia kept all our arrangements in order like a mother hen tending her chicks.

It is still a mystery today why the name Pajęczno was mentioned in previous notes. Not having found any trace of my family's name was a bit unnerving but I felt as if we were moving closer as we eliminated each possibility. We still had Rzeszów and Kolbuszowa to investigate. Meantime we could observe and absorb the essence of the country, as well as the beauty and history of Kraków.

"I'm crying with you, America

I am with you, America

I pray for you, America"

Hoot at the American Consulate office in Kraków following 9/11/01.

The American Consulate in Kraków was closed. Many notes were left by the Poles at the door; hundreds of candles and flowers filled the sidewalk in the next few days. People came and had their moment of silence. A young couple brought their child to place a rose among the rest of this outpouring of love and support in reaction to the 9/11 tragedy. An old woman bent to light a candle while another waited...telling Gosia she had also lit one. I thanked her and she was very pleased. She spoke no English, nor I Polish, but we understood.

Later as we were buying groceries I joked with the clerk although we didn't share the same language. It's easy to understand our simple daily behaviors across cultures. All women buying cheese or meat at the market behave pretty universally and we laughed at our similarities as the pointing and sign language continued. At the check-out the clerk asked Gosia where I was from. Gosia told her I was an American who lived just 3 hours from the NYC terror. She burst into tears and excused herself. Susan came along and asked what had happened. She went to the woman to give her a hug and the woman clung to her, crying. Such was our experience with these wonderful people. By the following day, the police had to close the street where the Consulate was. Hundreds of people gathered there to pray. Walking amongst them was awesome and inspiring. The candles and flowers now filled the street completely, reminding me of Weschler's[6] book describing this behavior when the Poles were oppressed by the Soviets who tried to eliminate certain religious or political holidays. No one has ever stopped this tide of sentiment. Word spreads without official radio or newspaper announcements and these people know what to do.

Our time in Kraków was glorious, from the Cloth Market to Wawel Castle to the small cafes along the way; it was as charming a city as we had ever seen. My Kraków pen pal, Joanna (a PhD. Student) was a proud guide, joining Gosia and us to rave about the World Heritage Square and architecture dating to

---

6   Weschler; Solidarity, The Season Of Its Passion

the 1200s. But this was an intermission in my search for grandfather's birthplace. We savored our time, said goodbye to our
English speaking guides, and loaded our bags onto a train bound
for Rzeszów and the next phase in my search.

The train passes through rural agrarian landscapes with lush
and laden pear trees reminding me of my grandfather. Rows
of vegetables are neatly tended; the soil is dark and rich. My
husband watches the passing forest in the hope of spotting deer.
These woods are plentiful and the game is offered on nearly
every restaurant menu. My Pennsylvania-born husband found
this point very appealing.

Joanna had given us instructions to watch a nearby passenger who was also bound for Rzeszów to know when we should
get off the train. It was an older woman who helped us and was
excited to tell her story to the family who met her at the station.
We didn't know a word she said but it was obvious they were all
tickled by the story. In Rzeszów we stayed in a Communist-era
hotel with small austere rooms that had hotel rules posted on
the door, written with a Communist tone. Rzeszów seemed more
of a businessman's town. A busy intersection for railway travel,
we used it as such and did a little investigation of its offerings.
We arranged for a taxi driver to take us to Kolbuszowa the following day. The desk clerk told us the driver enjoyed practicing
his English and we trusted her to give him a general idea of
what we were looking for. Michael turned out to be an agreeable
guy about 40 years old, who probably understood about ten per-
cent of what we were saying, but with plenty of sign language

and finding a few key words, we all got on very well. We first located the large Catholic church of Kolbuszowa, the most obvious place to begin our search. We felt lost without Gosia who

Michael the taxi driver

had returned to Warsaw; her translation skills are absolutely priceless. Susan and I headed for the priests' home with Michael while my husband crossed the street to find a cold drink at a tiny neighborhood store across the way. No one answered the door to the rectory, but I couldn't allow the search to end here. I sug-

gested we walk the cemetery to search for the family name. Michael understood and so the three of us entered the densely populated burial ground where you often climbed over tombs to get to the next row. Graves and monuments extend right up to the church wall and over the hill toward the street. There are no rows anymore, scarcely a place for a car to enter the newer section for a burial. Yet occasionally there is a new grave in the midst of the dense collection of stones, crosses, angels, saints and other monuments. We spread out in different directions, calling across to one another as we marveled at the tightly packed, yet well-tended headstones. Michael was the first to call out. He found a Rząsa stone! We rushed to see it, photograph it and squeal a bit in celebration of our joyous find. Now we were energized to scramble around more memorials until soon each

2001 · · · ·

of us was crying out with another find. All the Rząsa stones were photographed and we wrote all the information in my notebook. We were certain now that I had come to the place where my family had lived, died, married, farmed, or left behind when they packed off to the United States.

Kolbuszowa cemetery

In the meantime, my husband had made the acquaintance of the shop owner across the street. Coincidentally the man had lived in Brooklyn, NY for two years and spoke some English. He spoke of an old woman named Rząsa who came to the cemetery daily. He didn't know her full name or where she lived and with our minimal language skills, we concluded there was no way to explore the lead any further.

At lunch in the main square of Kolbuszowa, the waitress

was charmed with us as we stumbled through the menu with Michael. In this a tiny rural town, we are celebrities. Tourists would not be likely to travel here. We wondered if we were the first Americans who had visited their simple restaurant. Before we left, I showed the waitress my family tree thinking it was a universal design and pointed to my name as well as the Rząsa names of Kolbuszowa. I hoped she would know some of the family but the name was unfamiliar to her as well.

We visited a little museum village at the side of town. It had a collection of thatched roof homes and barns, windmills, fences and tools brought together from the surrounding area to offer a glimpse of country life in the 1800s. It was the same general plan as our Sturbridge Village or Plymouth Plantations. I was delighted to see their preservation efforts and wished for more traffic to support and enjoy their efforts. My imagination took me to my ancestors living this way in tiny simple log houses as Marcin's family worked the farms we passed. It was sort of a time warp where I lived in several eras simultaneously. This introduction to the culture of the 1800s Kolbuszowa acquainted me with the lifestyles of my grandparents prior to their leaving Poland. Without speaking the native tongue, I would have to be satisfied with that and the probability that I had found the right town out of the list of possibilities we had started with.

Early the next day we started our return journey back to Warsaw, tired of straining as we hauled our bags from one town, hotel or train to the next. Clicking along the tracks through peaceful countryside, there were cows scattered in each of their sections, as if by agreement. Stray goats and sheep near the train tracks seemed to have no fear. Sometimes the farms appeared out of proportion when compared to the humble little houses and lone farmer with primitive horse and cart, to care for all of it. One wonders how these gentle people could be called to war. They are such peaceful hard working people, who obviously love the land.

Sloping hills in the south flatten out as you approach Warsaw. We rolled through suburbs and into the city center, happy to be finished with transferring from town to town for a while. Returning to our Warsaw flat, familiar as it was, felt like a homecoming. We weary travelers were tickled with the treasures of clean clothes, food in the refrigerator, extra shoes and a washing machine! Chestnut trees with rusty leaves hung outside our apartment window looking down on the narrow cobblestone street heading toward Old Town. I loved seeing the neighbors' stucco houses washed with earthy tones of sienna and puce and topped with red tile roofs. A black and white cat positioned himself in an open window, lace curtains moving with the air. A church steeple could be seen above the roof tops. How many have we seen in this Catholic country? I thought about our visit to St. Mary's in Kraków where people come to pray at all hours of every day. There is always someone there: an old woman, a young man. They fall to their knees on the stone floor – even in the busy aisle just inside the door.

Gosia shared our final days in Old Town, bringing us parting gifts and delivering us to the airport in a cab. She couldn't have been a more generous ambassador. We planned for her to write (in Polish) to the Diocese in Rzeszów as well as the parish in Kolbuszowa, assuming my family's records would be housed there if they were from Kolbuszowa. It's hard to know if records were hidden in other cities because of invasions and whether they had been returned to the original town. There was also an effort to centralize information, but which churches had taken steps in that direction? Progress may not have reached the small parishes with limited resources. It would be a dream to think there would be a day when all these records would be digitized or even microfilmed.

And so our journey ended with still more affection for Poland and its people. I felt certain we had located the right village out of all the towns listed in my father's scraps of paper as well as in Uncle Peter's records. If Gosia's request for information was successful, we would finally have answers for my missing links in the family tree.

The confusion and high security resulting from 9/11 made our trip back to the States more cumbersome as each airport struggled with enforcing search methods and the delays they would incur. We were happy to be on U.S. soil again with all our friends intact and fortunate to have avoided feeling the brunt of the horror in New York.

2001

Bringing Home the news

I was excited to visit my Uncle Michael & Aunt Jenny when I returned home, to bring them my photos and news from Poland. These are average people who live in a clean unassuming bungalow with glitter in their plaster ceilings. We had a pleasant visit with lots of chatter about my trip to Poland as well as the usual stories about various members of our disconnected family.

Jenny was immediately taken with my photos of Poland – marveling at how beautiful the buildings were and how nice the whole place was overall. Her comment, "I thought it would be like all slums." She repeated her surprise a number of times. They paid strict attention to all of my descriptions as we went through each photo – and the book on Kolbuszowa. They thanked me over and over for coming and showing them what Poland looks like. Jenny is part Polish and part Ukrainian. She remembered stories of how poor everyone was and how rural it was – with no other houses around. She had a picture in her mind that was so different from what my pictures revealed. I was so glad I had taken the time to visit.

We drifted into a conversation about the family and all the "craziness" of Aunt Agnes and her daughters – Joey and his family – and finally to life in the Zosa family of Michael's youth. I told them I found information in a census book about my mother being in the state home for children. I asked if other children had been with her. I told them Nana had spoken of my grandmother's drinking and disappearing for days or weeks at a

1900s · · · · · 1920s · · · · · 1960s · · · · · 1970s · · · · · 1980s · · · · · 1990s

time. Once I told them I knew these stories, they began to open up with more on the subject. Michael immediately recalled being placed in a foster home with an Irish family. Jenny told of an incident where my grandmother was drunk getting off a bus with one of the babies and dropped the child in the snow as she went. "She dropped the baby getting off the bus... and just left him there." Jenny said. "The people yelled after her and the kids were taken away from her." "She was unfit," Michael added with a wistful sadness – that read as old pain. There was finality in his voice accompanied by a sigh...like the last exhale.

He said he remembered a day when she came after him saying, "Come with me to the police." He questioned why and she said "just come." When they reached the police station, she told the police she wanted them to bring her home so her husband wouldn't beat her. She had been gone for a week or two weeks and didn't want her husband to be mad and beat her. I couldn't picture my grandfather doing such a thing. I don't know if it was just the story of an alcoholic.

Michael said, "She would take the store book and buy things and she'd sell them to get money to buy whiskey or moonshine. Pa wouldn't discover it until he went to the grocery store to pay his bill. He had to keep the book away from her. It was a wonder that any of us lived through it. She was a lousy cook. She would be boiling something on the stove and wind up pouring in an entire box of salt. No one could eat it." More stories flowed. "There was no such thing as holidays – Christmas or Easter. I remember going to a hall for dinner at Christmas. We just hung

around there all day. That was Christmas. They'd give you a nice
meal and something for each kid. We got a dime once – and a
bag of candy." Jenny said my grandmother had a real mean
streak. "She wouldn't let Martin talk. As soon as he opened his
mouth, she'd yell at him." Michael said she drank right up to
the time he went into the Army in the early 40s. We wondered
when and why she stopped drinking. He didn't know. I said I
didn't recall her drinking when we went to visit (when I was
a kid) and they agreed. At some point – for some reason – it
stopped. We thought it may have coincided with the war years
and rationing – but there was really no information about that.

I pointed out that the ship's roster showed Martin being 25
years old and single. Aunt Jenny said, "Agnes always thought
there was something there, but who could believe anything she
said?" (There was a strained relationship between them and
Agnes.) Again the suspicions and doubts about my grandparents
and their arrival in this country. It was this absence of information which allowed for human nature to try and fill in the
blanks. No one ever expressed exactly what they were thinking
but I understood their inferences. The various siblings harbored
doubts about their parents' legal entry into the country, whether
they escaped from Galicia because of hard times, or could they
be Jews in disguise? Sometimes they wondered if there had been
a legal marriage. Too many details and dates left unrecorded
offered the opportunity to conjure up all sorts of explanations.
The parents obviously didn't explain or discuss much with their
children. The only story ever told was grandmother's stow-away

story and all their papers being burned. It was their refusal to go into detail and their behavior, when being questioned, that created this aura of mystery. It left everyone wondering why they didn't want to talk about it. My mother had behaved the same way when I questioned her about her childhood, so I could easily grasp what the Zosa siblings felt.

I was more determined than ever after our Poland trip. I was certain that Kolbuszowa must be the town where my grandparents were born. Now I would have to endure the wait while Gosia requested information from the Catholic Diocese in Rzeszów about Marcin Rząsa.

I have found that discovering one's roots can be a life altering process. A piece of information is discovered and it sometimes takes months for it to be thoroughly absorbed. And then the questions come. If this is true, then what about that? Then a light bulb goes on and I realize the connection or relevance to something else. It's a chain reaction – dominoes falling into place as the weeks tick by. Sometimes I am slow to fully absorb, and my next step cannot be taken until I am comfortable with my thoughts, my assimilation. Just as these immigrants had to adjust to our culture, I am reversing that process as I learn more about their culture and Poland's history. Someone described it as "straining to fathom the unique Polish soul."

2001 · · · ·

It doesn't take place in a vacuum, although I sometimes wish it could. My family, business, community involvement and other elements of my life pulled me from my focus for days and sometimes weeks. We sold our home of 32 years and moved back to the house I had grown up in – an antique from the 1700s, which consumed over a year in restoration work. This vintage home has always been my favorite and the added bonus is that I have been able to investigate my family history while living in a house that has cradled so many families' histories. My mother seems closer to me here. The room that was once her bedroom is now my study where I spend early morning hours reading or writing. Textiles and souvenirs of Poland are scattered in this room. I am surrounded by my Polish roots.

Third Trip to Poland

2003

Warsaw

❋

Kraków

❋

Kolbuszowa

❋

Cmolas

❋

Kazmierz Dolny

Months passed without a response from the Polish Diocese to Gosia's inquiries. I had become accustomed to this sort of disappointment. It was only a matter of time before I would lose patience waiting and find a way to return to Poland and continue the search in person.

In September of 2003 emails with Gosia describe the continuing fruitless efforts to document grandfather's life. We began to plan my return to Poland. "My plan at the moment is to do closings on two houses October 16 and then fly away as soon as possible. I may pause in England to catch my breath and adjust to the time change. I don't travel easily. Then off to Warsaw. I'd love to see your "almost new" flat and stay with you for a day or two. Then I'll take the train to Kraków. Will you come with me? I'm going to arrange to stay for two weeks. But who knows? I may be like Marisha (from Virtual Tourist[7]) who one day packed everything in her car and moved to Poland permanently! I don't think Hoot or the dog would appreciate that plan. I'm excited to be making more permanent arrangements and looking forward to seeing you soon."

Gosia replied, "I just wanted to let you know that I finally got a reply from the Rzeszów State Archives – did I mention I had emailed them again? They only said they didn't have the archives for Kolbuszowa so they forwarded my e-mail directly to the Kolbuszowa Civil Office. I think that's even better. "No reply from the Diocese archives, and having tried to call the All Saints parish for 2 days, I gave up, and then got busy again.

"Now for your trip to Poland....yeah, why don't you move here permanently? If you plan to be here at the break of October and November, you will have a unique chance to see the All Soul's Day on November 1. That's when people light candles at cemeteries to commemorate and pray for their loved ones, and

---

7   www.VirtualTourist.com: a web site with thousands of members/travelers from all over the world sharing information about their home and all the cities/countries they have visited.

the view of cemeteries in the evening is really breathtaking! This is a holiday (off work) and more people travel all over Poland on this occasion than they do for Christmas. Can you imagine?"

By October of 2003 there had been no answer to the translated letters Gosia sent to the Polish Diocese and parish of Kolbuszowa for me. We had concluded that the only way to find documentation for my grandparents' births, marriage and life in Poland would be for me to pack my bags and drag Gosia south to Kolbuszowa. This time I would travel alone from the States. By now I had several Polish contacts through the Virtual Tourist(VT) web site and plans were made to meet several of them in both Warsaw and Kraków.

Gosia met me at the airport and we reunited as if we'd been lifelong friends. I was to stay at Gosia's flat while we were in Warsaw. She owned a flat in a typical concrete high rise building constructed during the Communist era, located at the rim of the bustling city of Warsaw.

Up the elevator and unlock the door to find Peter! I wasn't aware of a roommate, but although surprised, I was charmed by Piotr (Peter). I later learned that Piotr was an old classmate Gosia had taken in, and too shy to attempt speaking English, Gosia translated his greetings. He loves Americans, their accents, and movie stars, especially Al Pacino and other movie mobster types. I think he would have liked a longer visit with the American woman, but his plan was to visit family and I would enjoy the use of his bedroom.

Gos and I talked for hours in her bright, efficient little flat. Finally we were off to Old Town to have delicious Polish food in a charming restaurant located, as it typical, in the cellar of one of the buildings on the main square. I slept soundly after so much travel and excitement, waking to church bells and Gosia fixing breakfast which was long and lazy with more coffee than anyone should drink.

Sunday in Chopin Park is where the Poles enjoy a stroll, peacocks wander loose and children can feed the red squirrels from their hands. We met the VT (Virtual Tourist) squad at the Chopin statue, took photos, walked under the umbrella of dense trees and enjoyed lunch at a nearby café. Everyone was welcoming and curious about my family search, travelling alone for such a distance. I felt like a curiosity, realizing not many American women my age would venture off to Eastern Europe on such an adventure as mine.

Back to the flat where Piotr charmed and fascinated me. He's an intensely religious man, visiting his church at least once daily, so his fascination with American movie stars and mobsters seems contradictory. He's totally engaging and delighted with my presence until Gosia tires of the translating and sends him to the balcony for a smoke.

Next day we boarded the train for Kraków where we met another VT internet acquaintance who owned a B&B in Kraków. We stayed for several days exploring the Cloth Market Square, and the Jewish sector of Kazmierz. We drank coffee in nearly every café on the square. At one internet café, we searched the internet for Kolbuszowa and Gosia showed me a page for the Skansen Village there. I had visited it with my husband and daughter on our last visit. There on the site was a photo of one of their typical icons fastened to a tree. I had photographed that very icon on my previous trip. Gosia read the Polish text which said it was given to Skansen Village by Josef Rząsa! I was dumbfounded.

So many coincidences have occurred during my search. I've taken them as signs that I was on the right track and destined to continue digging. Every indication was that Kolbuszowa was the town where we'd find the elusive records.

Kraków was great fun and filled with learning about Polish history and culture. One prearranged dinner was at the oldest restaurant in Kraków (1364) with "MattCrazy" (his name on VT) and his wife. It was a delicious dinner and an evening full of laughter, translations, and getting acquainted. Matt is actually an orthopedic surgeon... so not really "crazy" except for his mania for photography. We've remained friends for years through the internet emails and subsequent visits to Poland.

We visited the Jagiellonian University, the second oldest north of the Alps – only about 4 years younger than the one in Prague. Copernicus studied there as well as Pope John Paul II.

Our carefree time in Kraków came to an end and it was time
to push on to Kolbuszowa. I drove a rented car (Gosia has never
driven) and Gos became my navigator reading the Polish maps
and road signs.

In Kolbuszowa we began our search at the cemetery where
we had previously found the family name of Rząsa on several
stones. It was late October and the Poles had begun the work of
cleaning cemeteries in anticipation of their widely celebrated
All Saints Day on November 1. Women bring buckets and scrub
brushes to clean the monuments. Most arrive on foot, some by
bicycle, and everyone is involved in the preparation for such an
important day. Ancestors will be remembered with hundreds
of flowers and candles in colored glass jars at every cemetery
throughout Poland.

We visited the convenience store across the street owned by
the man who had spent several years living in Brooklyn years
ago, and he remembered my husband from our last trip. He
referred to a man named Rząsa with a bakery in Green Point,
Brooklyn, as he had on the previous trip. He made some phone
calls to help us find anyone named Rząsa, but we found the
name was rare even here. A woman at the store corrected the
spelling of grandmother's name as FILUBA, not WIELUBA.
I'm always amazed that the Poles seem to know what the correct
spelling of a name should be. It's so unlike the United States
where you are likely to find names spelled different ways due
to changes in spelling when the family arrived in America, as
was the case with my family.

Helpful Priest

The priest who answered the door at the rectory next to the cemetery explained to Gosia that we should try another church in nearby Cmolas, where some old records would be kept. There was some explanation about Kolbuszowa being split and he was too busy with preparations for the coming holiday to be of any further help to us. He let us know his time was precious and it would not include probing old books for my ancestors. Gosia was polite and respectful. We moved on.

I had learned of a museum cared for by an old woman in Kolbuszowa, but all we found was a note on the door and further disappointment.

We probed the area for a few leads we'd been given, found nothing helpful, had dinner in the only restaurant in the square, strangely named the Krokodyl Restaurant, and stayed in a horrid hotel where there was no heat or hot water. We froze all night, sleeping in our clothes. Gosia gave the desk clerk quite a tongue lashing in the morning and refused to pay the full rate for the room. I chuckle to myself at her assertiveness. She has no tolerance for sub-standard service and seems embarrassed for me to see her countrymen's lack of graciousness. Much of the countryside and small towns in Poland are simply not set up for tourists. This hotel was typically used by students who came for athletic events and we were there in an off-season. There were no alternatives, so we were forced to adapt, but not without a bit of rage on Gosia's part, finding their behavior and

2001 · · · · 2003 · · · · ·

accommodations inexcusable. I relate this to you, dear reader, to give fair warning that you cannot expect to find all the conveniences of a more developed town when you are digging for your roots in the hinterlands of Poland.

We pressed forward following the directions of the priest which took us to the village of Cmolas. We found the rather new church and priests' home just a few miles outside of Kolbuszowa. A frail older priest in simple black vestments answered the door of the rectory and brought us in from the frigid wind. He ushered us through a dimly lit hallway and into a small office that barely held a desk and two chairs where we sat to discuss our request and my reason for travelling from America. He listened carefully while asking few questions. His face showed no emotion, no clues to his inner thoughts. He agreed to search a few books, explaining he wasn't the priest who would usually deal with such matters. His demeanor was totally unlike the younger priest in Kolbuszowa who so hastily discouraged a search and clarified that his time was precious. No, this man knew his responsibility for the records of an earlier time, a time in which the church kept the only records of a family's existence before city halls and census takers.

Slowly he took one ledger after another from the shelf in an adjoining room. I watched his hands as he opened a random page, scanning the old lists of births on the yellowed pages. We watched as he investigated several books with careful reverence for their importance. He rose to find another book and when he returned with that edition, he didn't have very many pages to turn before he quietly began to read the entries. Although he was reading in Polish, I hung on the words, holding my breath as he spoke. The pale arthritic finger moved down row after row of entries. I listened for recognizable words.

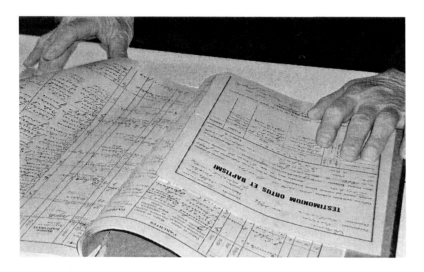

First I heard "Rząsa," then "Piotr," then "Marcin" a few more words and then "Marianna." I yelped, but he was unaffected by my joy. Gosia was scribbling the information and translating as quickly as she wrote. Her gift for thinking in two languages simultaneously is often mind boggling. What he had found was confirmation of a legitimate birth and further mention of the parents and grandparents being born in this parish. Once again, our intro into the data we searched for was provided by that uncooperative Uncle Peter — Piotr Rząsa, born February 9, 1905, in Zarębki, Kolbuszowa.

We didn't have the date of marriage or exact birth dates of my grandparents, but the record mentioned the couples' ages at the birth. This quiet man went patiently about the business of searching announcements of marriage for several years prior until he found the 3rd posting of the intent to marry, giving us the bride and groom's parents' names as well. Now we knew that Marcin was the son of Józef Rząsa and Magdalena Skowron. Marianna Filuba was the daughter of Antoni Filuba and Apolonia Kosiorowski of Mechowiec. I was in shock. It seemed extraordinary that I should have such a windfall of information after so many years of erroneous little scraps. And so 97 years after Marcin Rząsa's arrival in the U.S. his granddaughter who smiled through the kitchen window on Derry Street as a child, had found her way back to this remote corner of Poland to discover the roots of the family. We arranged for official documents to be sent to Gosia and a mass to be said for Marcin and Marianna. He asked if I would be attending the mass, but Gosia explained I would be back in the States by then. He suggested the mass be said for Marcin, Marianna and the *entire* family... to which I agreed. I thought of Uncle Michael knowing about his family and our roots. I would notify the entire family that on this Christmas a mass would be said for all of our family in this native land.

Thank goodness Gosia was there to help me through not only the translation, but my astonishment at finally finding evidence of my family's existence. I can't explain what all of this meant to me. I have no words to describe my joy.

The priest had questions about my homeland. He was curious if the priests still wore vestments and if there were Polish priests in the U.S. I explained that Nana grew up in a Polish parish and had mass in Polish. There are other Polish priests scattered around the state along with parishes made up of many Polish people. He seemed quietly happy to know the priests are there somewhere... saying the mass in all their vestments.

We thanked him over and over but he was unmoved by our excitement. He couldn't know how long I had searched and how much this meant to me. He couldn't have imagined what it was like to live in the West without access to information about your family, the culture, the country! He knew only his own side of Communism and the simple little village where he prayed. I left a donation for the mass to be said on Christmas morning, 2003.

So there it was. We had the answers. The priest would forward official documents to Gosia and she in turn would mail them to me in the States. My head was spinning and we were so busy digesting this new information, that we left the priest and village without asking anything further. The architecture of the church and rectory indicated that it had been built around the 1960s. There was a huge outdoor altar and seating area behind the large modern day brick church. It obviously was not the church of my grandfather, which we just assumed must have burned or was somehow destroyed years before. We should have questioned the priest about the former church, but we were too excited to think rationally.

Driving north along narrow roads bordered by groves of birch trees, my mind was filled with thoughts of grandfather and what life was like in his youth. We passed beautiful old peasant farms, horses, cows, barley fields, corn fields, cabbage fields and mistletoe growing high in the old deciduous trees. Sometimes we were slowed to a crawl following a farmer's horse cart filled with turnips. I found myself enjoying the moment so different from being stuck behind a slow vehicle on the roads at home. The cart and equipment used by many of these farmers is crude but pure. The air has no fumes from diesel. There were no chemicals sprayed on these fields, no hormones fed to their animals.

I emailed home to report our progress as soon as we got to our next stop. "It took 4.5 hours to drive here from Kolbuszowa, which was much longer than I expected. The farmers are beautiful. Wish I could have photographed more of them with their horse drawn wagons. Houses differed as we got into small country towns. This was more interesting than the train ride. I even learned that mistletoe grows in the top of their trees! Never saw it growing before. Almost looks like a squirrel's nest at a distance." I reported on our findings at the Cmolas church, proclaiming, "It's the REAL THING! And we were only about 4 miles away when we were there the last time. The original old wooden church is gone and there is a modern structure. We saw the man in the little store across the street from the church where we visited last time and he said to say hello to my husband and he wished him good health. He and the woman at the store gave us a couple of leads and again mentioned a Rząsa in Brooklyn with a bakery.

I had many stories to tell, notes in my journal, and photos in my new camera. I was about on overload now. I can't tell you how happy I was to finally find the end of the road. So many questions were answered. I was particularly eager to give Uncle Michael the news and information. It took from 1906 when Marcin Rząsa arrived in the United States until 2003 when his granddaughter finally discovered where they came from. I think Nana is happy too. She kept saying "Why don't you give it up, Jan?" Now she would say, "I can't believe it. Only Janet would do that." I'm glad I was able to live to do it and have the means and opportunity.

Kazmierz Dolny

We visited Kazmierz Dolny, a precious old town which commonly hosts lots of artists and summer visitors. I enjoyed its market day when the neighboring farmers bring their crops to the cobblestone square to sell and take the opportunity to chat with neighbors and townspeople. One farmer with sacks of grain for sale by the kilo struck me as typical of what members of my family must have looked like when they went to market day. Gosia translated that I wanted to photograph him and he resisted because he didn't have his good clothes on. We assured him this was the photo I wanted and I clicked my camera as he blushed.

It was a relief to be back in Gosia's flat. Peter was tickled to have us with him again. Gos and I shared dinner preparation and I introduced them to applesauce which they loved. Gosia translated my documents for me and we searched the internet for information about the church in Cmolas. It has been designated as a "sanctuary" which I had many questions about. Peter struggled to explain how they are established. I had known the word in the context of a bird sanctuary – a protected place – or at church, the part

The bashful farmer with bags of grain at market day in Kazmierz Dolny

of the altar where the host was kept. Peter's use of the words "sanctum sanctorum" was to describe a holy of holies place. In Poland, many miracles are recognized and remembered with a pilgrimage, or religious journey sometimes taking many days to complete. Perhaps the most notable example of this is the enormous pilgrimage to Our Lady of Częstochowa annually. Gosia described the legions of believers who travel on foot in their devotion. That pilgrimage is to recognize the miraculous icon of the black Madonna, which we visited when I searched Częstochowa on our previous trip. I am still unclear about the reference to that city in my father's notes.

In Cmolas, the acknowledged miracle involves a young boy's vision of the transfiguration which he produced in a painting later in his life. It hangs in the church where the miracle occurred in 1585. I was intrigued by the story and the opulence of the site. The part that continues to mystify me is the grandness of this 1960s church, amphitheater for outdoor worship, and the priests' rectory. The size and impressiveness of the sanctuary seemed so out of proportion with the size and economics of the village and parish. Gosia assured me that gifts and donations from all the pilgrims would account for the church's ability to build such a shrine. Amazing when you consider the 1960s under Communism in Poland.

My days in Poland came to an end and it was time to travel home with hundreds of memories and happy thoughts of my good fortune. I now began to feel torn between two homelands. I couldn't have asked for greater blessings than Gosia's friendship, my opportunity to explore Poland, and that sweet priest finding the answers to my very long search.

Flying home, I sat beside a man named Witek (pronounced vee-tek) who was curious about my constant scribbling and

asked if I was writing a book. We talked about my search and he was amazed because he lives in Kolbuszowa and was married in grandfather's old wood church! He described the church being moved from its original location and went on to relate that local people didn't like the "big priest" in that parish. He claimed that the townspeople called him "mafia" because he had lived in NYC for several years during Communism and Poles there gave him money for their families in Kolbuszowa which was never received on the other end. He said, "I'm sorry, but that is what everyone said." He spoke of his home and family in Poland and explained he travels to Brooklyn, NYC for work 5 or 6 months every year to earn money, returning home to enjoy the Polish summer with clean air and wholesome, pure foods. By the way, the work Witek did in the States was painting Jewish synagogues, of all things. He said the job sometimes took two years to complete and I understood his description to mean he was doing decorative painting as opposed to simply rolling the paint across a wall.

He said he knew the man in the convenience store across from the church in Kolbuszowa and also knows of a man by the name of Rząsa who owns a bakery in the Green Point neighborhood of Brooklyn. We exchanged contact information and vowed to stay in touch. Witek would call the man at the bakery to help me find a connection to family. It began to feel as if I were part of a tightly knit community.

You can imagine my mind was blown by the end of this trip. I had peeled back many layers of time and absorbed so much information, history and culture, that I found myself checking under my fingernails for Polish dirt, half expecting myself to suddenly begin speaking in the native tongue.

And what was that story of the wooden church being moved all about?

Return to U.S. and more adventures

In the meantime, the connection between Gosia and I continued through emails as we reviewed what we had covered, what we were missing and what we would do about it.

I called Witek in NYC. He was working for the same boss he had the last year. He volunteered that he would visit the man in the bakery the next weekend and get back to me after that. He was convinced I would return to Poland the next year so that they could host my visit (along with Gosia) and help me to find family.

My friends, Marianne and Sam said, "Of course you have to go back! You've established a relationship now. You must go back." "I don't know if my old body can take much more of this shuffling from continent to continent," I thought. "However, it was very sweet of this man to offer so much. Perhaps I will return to Cmolas and grandfather's church one day."

I went to visit Uncle Michael and Aunt Jenny and they were thrilled in their own quiet way. They are ordinary people who don't get ecstatic about anything…but I knew they were

very happy to have me come and report all my findings. They thanked me repeatedly. Aunt Jenny kept saying how amazed she was that Poland had so much and was so CLEAN! She compared it to some of our areas with litter in the streets. She never imagined Poland to be so beautiful. She had had the same reaction to the photos from my last trip. We all laughed about Peter supplying the needed clues. There was a lot of absorbing of information going on which probably continued long after I left. Once finished with all of my stories I sat a long time as they remembered the miseries of the family. They feel that only Michael and my mother turned out well. Michael said, "I still don't know how any of us lived through it. I really don't." Their memory of grandmother is still too painful and vivid. I'm afraid no amount of information or pretty pictures will ever erase that unhappiness. They wished my mother was still here as she would have loved to hear all of this. I know that's true, but I feel as if she was with me on my trip. She always is.

It's a funny thing about losing your parents. They never really leave you. I always remembered something the priest said several times over in my father's funeral mass. "I am my father, and he is me." It's true for my mother and my father. Maybe that is what hurts Michael so much as well. I don't mean to be morbid. They were happy that I came and delighted to have the copies of the documents I gave them. Aunt Jenny was pleased I brought one of the Polish souvenir ceramic crosses and she said she would hang it right away. I knew they would have many interesting thoughts in the days to come, as I have had. At moments like these, after my meetings with Uncle Michael, I became more determined to complete my book to tell the story of this family and my search.

> Desalvo[8] writes, "They write about what they have lived through – experiences that might not be commonly known – to heal themselves. But they also write to help heal a culture that if it is to become moral, ethical, and spiritual, must recognize what these writers have observed, experienced, and witnessed.
>
> Writing testimony, to be sure, means that we tell our stories. But it also means that we no longer allow ourselves to be silenced or allow others to speak for our experience. Writing to heal, then, and making that writing public, as I see it, is the most emotional, psychological, artistic, and political project of our time."

It was the day a mass was to be dedicated to Marcin Rząsa and his family. I tried to notify as many family members as possible to tell them about the mass and the time difference between here and there so we might all be united in some way at that hour. Cards were returned as undeliverable from my Cousin Joey's son, Joe, Jr., and Cousin Dorothy, members of Aunt Agnes' family. I have no idea of their whereabouts or even if Dorothy survived her battle with cancer.

I went to 9 AM service at Trinity Church in Pawtuxet and met my daughter Susan there. The service was filled with

---

8   *Writing As A Way of Healing-How Telling Our Stories Transforms Our Lives, by Louise Desalvo, 2000

wonderful hymns and the church was decorated with dozens
of poinsettias wrapped with red ribbon bows. I told Susan about
waking in the early hours thinking about the mass, my grandfather, and the entire family. She said she sat straight up in
bed at 2 AM with the same thoughts. I felt my mother and
grandparents' spirits had come to us, gratefully acknowledging
my gesture. I was so moved as I thought about the family — its
years of problems over three generations of poverty and discon-
nection. I thought about the strength of that Polish faith I have
witnessed, and I remembered the gentle priest who found my
family's records. I prayed that all the mistakes the family has
made — the terrible deeds remembered — would all be forgiven
and each member blessed with peacefulness and light in their
lives — or deaths — wherever they were. And when I envisioned
this dysfunctional family and the strength of that Polish mass
of prayer — I welled up to overflowing. Susan asked, "What?
Why?" and I answered "It's just them. It's just them." It was all
I could say or describe as I sobbed. I was referring to the family
but all of the Poles as well. I felt as if the power of those Polish
prayers pulled at each of us at that moment. I can't describe the
depth of the Polish devotion, but all of what I've seen, heard,
read and felt about their unshakeable faith came to me that
Christmas. I am in awe of that spirituality — that oneness of
mind and faith which has saved the Polish culture and nation
from annihilation in the face of so many conquerors. I carry
those genes and feel that strength of will which I so wish I could
describe to you.

I've mentioned before that when you are doing a family search, you have to be ready for the unexpected moment when the phone rings in the middle of your busy day and no matter where your head was a moment before, you are suddenly whiplashed back in time to a family connection dating back fifty years. One morning I was preparing to go out with my daughter, who was about 15 minutes late. The dog barked to tell me someone was at the back door. I assumed it was Susan. When the dog continued her barking, I realized someone else was at the door. I was presented with a stranger. A man in his 60s, who immediately announced himself as Larry Czeczot! He was very rushed, explaining that he had someone waiting in the car, but he wanted to stop briefly to introduce himself. He insisted on producing his driver's license as identification to prove his validity. I didn't doubt his word, thinking, "How would anyone else ever devise a name like that connecting to a name like mine?" He was very anxious to give me all the information he could, as fast as he could. Rattling off names of siblings, parents, uncles, and cousins, he reviewed much of the information he had given me previously on the phone. I watched the expressions on his face, trying to identify a family "look" that fleetingly passed as he spoke. He told me Ann Czeczot was still living in Central Falls, but her health was failing. I recently sent a card to her when I discovered her name still listed in the phone book. I tried to remember if I had sent him one when I sent the card to Ann. I didn't think I had, but yet he arrived at my door, so what else would have inspired his visit?

Susan came to pick me up when Larry was preparing to leave and I was able to introduce them. He was talking very fast and trying to hurry back to his colleague waiting in the car. I thanked him for stopping and invited him to come again — perhaps with his wife to share my photos and information about Poland. He said he might but not in the near future. Again I sensed that he had some hesitation about his wife knowing anything about me or our meeting. He was gone before I could say much more and I thought, "This wouldn't have happened if Susan hadn't been that 15 minutes late."

Reflecting later I thought how strange these things are. He must have wanted to connect, making the effort to stop in the middle of his work day. Strange that he came past the front door, up the walk to the back porch to knock at the back door to my kitchen. It's a family entrance. Most strangers would have knocked at the front door. It was as if he had been here before. It made me wonder if he had come here previously, although my mother never mentioned him visiting. We had moved to my family's house in the interim since my initial conversation with Czeczot on the phone. Perhaps he had driven past or come by when no one was at home. He obviously had been thinking about our relationship and made a real effort to connect.

Larry is a 62 year old man who is retired from "the International brotherhood of the Teamster," he reported. He works for Enterprise Car Rental and was delivering cars when he stopped to see me. He said he didn't stay in touch with his brothers who were in Florida. I would return to my computer to search for his brothers. If I could engage any of them in conversation, I might learn more about their grandmother and her connections to my grandfather. I did have a moment to slip in the piece of information from Gosia re: the mystery of our grandparents being step-sister and brother. I wasn't sure if he followed it (he was in such a hurry!) but I was clear that our grandparents were first cousins.

Larry Czeczot paid me a surprise visit once again on a Sunday morning. He had a little more time to visit and so he sat in my kitchen having coffee and smoking cigarettes. I tried to interest him in my maps, photos and book of Kolbuszowa. He didn't seem terribly curious about my adventures in Poland or the Family Tree, but rather wanted to have a visit with someone who would share his melancholy for old ethnic connections. I think he speaks a bit of Polish and may long for conversation in that tongue. I invited him to return for my photo exhibit when Gosia came to visit. He might enjoy speaking Polish with her.

We reviewed everything we had covered previously. They had lived next door to his grandmother (Agnes[9]) and he shared a few of his childhood memories of her. He said she was a very

---

9   Agnes was grandfather's "step sister" as they referred to her in my family. My aunt Agnes may have been named for her.

quiet woman who kept to herself. When the boys played ball and hit it into her yard, she would retrieve it. The boys would have to go to see her in order to get the ball back. He added another minor detail that his grandmother was a tiny woman less than 5 feet tall. This coincides with my grandfather being only about 5 feet tall and my mother, who was 4 feet 11 inches tall. It was obviously a genetic family trait.

My husband came in during our visit and they seemed to enjoy meeting, so I thought we could expect further visits. Larry verified information about his brothers, who live in Florida. Later I emailed the newspaper in Daytona Beach where his brother is an Editor. I hoped to make another connection and perhaps find more memories. Larry had an older brother, retired from a position where he "designed jet airplanes," as Larry explained. It was an interesting coincidence that my son, Christopher, manages a corporate jet, and was schooled in Daytona at Embry Riddle Aeronautical University.

There are times when I'm not actively engaged in the investigation of documents and archives – yet I still find myself collecting the culture of my ancestors by whatever means available. One such occasion was my adventure with my son Christopher, and his wife Karen, into Brooklyn to find Witek. He is the man who flew home from Poland with me and was married in my grandfather's church in Cmolas. Today his life consists of working six months in Brooklyn to earn enough money to support his family and then he returns to his agrarian home outside Kolbuszowa for the balance of the year.

While in Brooklyn, Witek rents a small apartment in which he says he lives "like an animal." The 4th floor walk-up takes you through dismal hallways made of rugged materials to withstand the wear without the necessity of maintenance, for it has none. Cleaning agents and paint are foreign to these bleak staircases. We entered a narrow hall with storage bins piled along the wall and were directed to the first room on the right. It was the bedroom/living room/all-purpose space in which we found worn, unmatched old pieces of furniture he had collected from the street or cast off from other residents to provide the basics for his six months stay in this place which was scarcely more than hovel.

A dirty window offered sunlight to the room and a box against the wall became the table where Witek excitedly accumulated cups, cheesecake, fried dough, and his substitute for sugar, black currant syrup. He insisted this was better for your heart and circulation than the processed sugar most Americans use. He rushed from a nearby kitchen to our meeting room bringing all his delicacies while urging us to be comfortable, please. So happy to share his simple quarters with his charm and generous nature, you could forget what he was missing in material goods. He came to rest sitting on an empty plastic bucket left from his work in the city.

We looked at photos of his home in Poland, his children, wife, and other "familia" members. He told the stories of his years of military service under Communism and we laughed at his stories of how the Polish men worked on planes with careless abandon (sabotage?) while ignoring attempts to brainwash them into Communist thinking. He said he managed to escape, finding his way into the US Air Force "working as a spy and later being released to travel the world freely as an American citizen." It is still unclear how he could have accomplished all of this and I am sure there are missing pieces to his stories, but somehow it doesn't matter. What you get from listening to the stories, the apologies for his humble surroundings and his obvious delight to have company in his home is the essence of his Polish nature. All that I read of their – no, *our* history – is so consistent with that special element that permeates the culture without exception. They are consistently Polish, through and through. In this country of multi-cultural families, we seldom find so pure a strain of ethnic identity as I have found in these Polish friends in my search for family.

Witek produced a phone book listing all businesses and residential addresses & phone numbers of Polish people in the U.S. He spoke of being ashamed & embarrassed for not searching out the Rząsa who owns the bakery in Brooklyn as he had said he would. He stressed that Saturday wasn't a good day to find this man. He would be too busy in his shop and we would be arriving unannounced. He preferred to take the next three weeks to locate the shop, the man, and make some initial contact – before we all descended on him, asking for history and family connections. I was disappointed but agreed he was no doubt accurate in his assessment. He was so concerned I might be angry after traveling such a distance, that his apologies repeated ten times over – even to his pleading with Chris and Karen while I was out of the room to please make me understand and not be angry with him. Of course I told him I couldn't be angry and I understood his position.

Our visit concluded with Witek emptying cupboards and drawers to give us container after container of nails and screws taken from his jobs, which he had intended to send back to Poland. Of course, when he investigated the cost of postage, he realized his error. He insisted that since we were about to undertake further work on our house, we would put these supplies to good use and save ourselves money. There were rolls of masking tape for wall board and a variety of items which were then packed into another white bucket for transport to Rhode Island. The giving continued with his packaging up all the cheesecake and Polish donuts left from our afternoon visit, as well as his insistence that we carry back the apple cake we had brought to him. It didn't end there. He rushed to some drawers where he found packages of Polish cookies and candies which he packed into yet another plastic bag. It took the four of us to haul all of this down the four flights of stairs to the trunk of the car where we all said "good bye" and wished one another good health and promised to meet again soon as my search for my Polish roots continued.

I am reminded of the book *Solidarity; Poland in the Season of Its Passion* written by the New Yorker Magazine author, Lawrence Weschler when he speaks of the Polish nature. He tells of the severe shortages and poverty of Poland which were part of the impetus for the Solidarity movement. He said while traveling in the country he noted all the Poles generously offering cigarettes to anyone they met or to a stranger approaching on the street. He watched the generosity repeatedly while wondering how they could afford all these cigarettes during bleak times when hardly a pack could be found on any store's shelf! He finally asked a Pole how could it be, and the answer came, "Simple. There are no matches!" Polish humor at its finest. And a good glimpse of that nature which has me enamored of them.

I contacted Larry Czeczot's brother Michael in Florida hoping he could offer childhood memories or information collected from the Czeczot family but, "as my brother Larry may have mentioned, my Mom and Dad were divorced shortly after my birth. Most of my childhood/early teen family memories are built around my Mom's side of the family." "I know how important the smallest 'kernel' of information is (have been a journalist since '75, and was a private investigator with Pinkerton's for a time before that), but, honestly, can't remember anything that would even remotely resemble a 'seed', much less anything that would 'bear fruit'. Good luck in your efforts! – Mike"

In 2004 and 2005 Larry Czeczot paid several unexpected visits to me. Unfortunately he had little to offer about the family and enjoyed telling me stories about his career as a truck driver which had now morphed into delivering cars for a car rental agency. These near constant discussions of driving led to the story about his car, which needed repair and he was short on money to reclaim it, so he wanted to borrow $20. The first time it was startling and embarrassing, but I loaned the money. When it took 3 visits to return the $20 followed by several months and then another visit requesting another loan of $20, I decided this would be a family tree branch I would not care to nurture. I refused the loan, Larry left and there were no further visits or family discussions. I was reminded of the way my grandfather's relationship with the family back in Poland dissolved following Victoria's careless remark.

Just as disappointments dot the landscape of family searching, so do rays of sunshine. In March of 2004 I had a welcome email from Gosia. "Hi Janet, Hey, I got something from the parish in Cmolas today: three records for you!! Isn't that JUST GREAT?? All three are signed by father Józef Żółtek, and if I am not mistaken, he is the one who wrote the copy of your uncle's baptismal record when we were there in October. He's sent baptismal records of Marcin and Marianna, as well as their marriage record. Here's what they say:"

2001 · · · · 2003 · · · ·

Marcin Rząsa

Record of Baptism (1877 #23, Vol. IV, p.132)

Name of father: Józef, son of Wojciech and Marianna Rolek

Name of mother: Magdalena, daughter of Jan Skowron and Marianna Pyra

Birth date & place: 16 Oct 1877, Zarębki

Baptism date & place: 16 Oct 1877, Cmolas

Marianna Fieluba

Record of Baptism (1882 #7, Vol. V, p.87)

Name of father: Antoni

Name of mother: Apolonia Kosiorowska

Birth date & place: 5 Mar 1882, Mechowiec

Baptism date & place: 5 Mar 1882, Cmolas

Marcin and Marianna

Marriage Certificate (1903#3, Vol. III, p.70)

Bridegroom: Marcin Rząsa, Catholic, resident of Zarębki,

Born on 16 Oct 1877 in Zarębki

Bride: Marianna Fieluba, Roman-Catholic, resident of Mechowiec,

Born on 5 Mar 1882 in Mechowiec

"I think these are the three that we asked them for, remember? We left them a little list and here we are. Would you like me to mail them to you or shall I just bring them with me? Would you like me to write something to that priest on your behalf? Plus, I still have the $50 that you sent some time ago to cover some search cost. If this is what you'd like to donate, I'll send them the money. Just let me know what you'd like, OK? I'm so happy for you! Gosia"

Such a bonanza of information! The donation to the church could scarcely convey my gratitude to that sweet priest who so responsibly fulfilled my request. There is no way to express my thankfulness to him.

That winter was when Gosia and I began to plan for her trip to the U.S. She worried about being able to obtain a visa at first but had no problem because she owned property in Poland and had a job with a more than average income. She concluded that these considerations would weigh heavily in her not becoming a burden in the States, and having substantial reason to return home. Many other Poles were slowed for months or denied a visa entirely at that time.

Gosia would fly into Newark, N.J. airport, which isn't far from where my son Christopher and wife Karen lived. I drove to their house; we gathered Gosia and spent a couple of days running in and out of the city, which of course included Ellis Island. The intermix of the city's density and the relaxed atmosphere of Chris and Karen's patio in the evening was a perfect solution for a whirlwind tour of New York.

2001 . . . . 2003 . . . . .

Gos got a real taste of freeway driving on the way back to R.I., so different from the roads we travelled between Warsaw and Kraków. We spent the next couple of weeks visiting Providence, Boston, Rockport, Gloucester, Plymouth, Newport, and we even flew to Washington, D.C. for a few days. We packed in as much as our energy would allow, and Gosia loved it all – from beaches, to city, to monuments and mansions. Similar to the way I enjoy morning coffee on her balcony, she enjoyed her morning coffee on the back porch with Hoot. We loved having her here and hearing her impressions of my village and our country. We had now reversed our roles. One observance she made was how many people display the American flag here. It was especially true following the 9/11 events. She said it was rare in Poland where after years of being restricted from 'showing your colors' the practice never took hold. When she returned home she began proudly flying the Polish flag from her balcony.

It was sad to part with my special friend when she left and again I marveled at how comfortable we were travelling and living together. I'm old enough to be her mother but we interact on a more level plane. She is a joy in my life.

Reminders of my mother's childhood and the Zosa family sometimes caught my attention when I least expected it and inspired me to push on with my search. A *Providence Journal*

newspaper article about the "State Home and School, the former state dormitory for orphans" appeared in the local paper at the opening of 2005. It described a project to restore the gates and superintendent's house, creating a research center. The orphanage had closed its doors 25 years earlier and now there was a move to recognize all the children who had moved through the system and hear the stories of their past. The superintendent's mansion was restored and archeologists excavated buttons, toys, marbles, and tongs from the old ice house. Nine decades of orphanage records uncovered the story of RI being among the first states to support a public orphanage. "It was after the Civil War, and certain parts of the country found they had a lot of widows and mothers who could not care for their children," said Hillman, the researcher. "It was also during this period that a huge number of immigrants were coming into the country, and private orphanages simply couldn't bear up under the weight."

And so the call went out to all the former residents of the center to participate in an oral history project to tell their stories of what it was like to be a ward of the state.

These reminders of my mother's past were bittersweet. I was glad that RI College and the State were giving recognition to the thousands of children who had the misfortune of having to live in such an institution, yet at the same time I felt the sting of my mother's wounds. I wondered what she would think about this noble project and knew she would hate to be reminded of those dismal years.

2001 · · · · · 2003 · · · ·

Fourth Trip
to Poland

2006

Warsaw

Gdańsk

Baranów Castle

Cmolas

Sandomierz

The 2006 trip was planned so that Gosia and I could find grandfather's old church and try to sort out our confusion about the three churches of Cmolas. We hoped to locate Witek's family along our way and some time would be spent discovering Warsaw with a side trip to Gdańsk and Sopot on the coast of the Baltic. Gosia's familiarity with the city along with her translation skills made it easy to move around as if I were a native.

I don't worry about going to Poland alone when I have such a competent Polish friend to travel with while I'm there. Another benefit is her vast knowledge of history which helps to interpret each site and post-war reconstruction. She was rightfully proud and excited to bring me to one of Poland's recent museums which drew from the latest interactive designs in America's [Smithsonian] museums. The Warsaw Uprising Museum graphically tells the 1944 story of the Polish insurgents who tried to save Warsaw, bravely fighting the German Army while Stalin's army stood across the Vistula waiting for Warsaw to fall. The insurgents and civilians (some Jewish members included) suffered from famine and the lack of effective help from the rest of the world.

American airdrops of supplies and food were not enough to sustain the Poles' growing hunger, depression, and solitude. The area defended by insurgents grew smaller each day. Capitulation was imminent.

More than 18 thousand insurgents and 180 thousand civilians died in the Uprising of 1944. Survivors were sent to concentration camps or deported to Germany to forced labor camps. The Germans carried out their long planned action of destroying Warsaw. Bombing continued for days and days until the city was reduced to ashes. The hope for Poland's independence had been ruled out at the Yalta Conference by the USA, Soviet Union and Great Britain as they bartered for Poland's future.

Following WWII and Soviet occupation, the Poles were not allowed to recognize, memorialize or acknowledge the events of

those days. Communist authorities spread propaganda to erase the Rising from social memory. Some insurgents were arrested and put in the same cells as German War Criminals. Finally after years of suppression, and the fall of the Soviet Union, people of Poland can tell their story and recognize the insurgents for their bravery and sacrifice. Karen Majewski writes in *Traitors and True Poles*, "In Poland, where borders have been dissolved, Poles are compelled to carry their nation within, internalizing the criteria by which they themselves distinguish themselves." At the Uprising Museum they finally tell their story to the world. When visiting Warsaw – go to this museum. You will find it a compelling and powerful site which tells a long overdue story.

We settled into the train to Gdańsk watching the changes in landscape as we travelled north. Tiny settlements were scattered among corn fields, compared to the hay fields of the south. Birch and pine trees fell away to poplar and maple and then fruit trees. Such great expanses of countryside.

Gdańsk's old town with its beautiful architecture sits quietly at the edge of the river which flows to the Baltic Sea. This is the coast where the first shot was fired commencing World War II. We ate, drank and giggled as we walked the old streets enjoying the vendors selling their amber jewelry and other souvenirs. St. Mary's Street and Long Street are lined with stunning Gothic buildings standing shoulder to shoulder on each side of the narrow cobbled streets. A violinist played classical music under an archway near the river.

(1900s) · · · · · (1920s) · · · · · (1960s) · · · · · (1970s) · · · · · (1980s) · · · · · (1990s)

We visited the Lenin Shipyard and Solidarity Museum
marked by a plaza with a powerful and symbolic steel structure. Stark and rugged, three obelisks rise to become crosses
several stories above street level. As they rise from the concrete
they appear to be breaking through the stone base, lifting the
pavement as if a groundswell were happening, a groundswell
of the peoples' revolt pushing up from the very earth. "The
monument was unveiled in 1980 to commemorate the events of
1970 when 45 people died during street riots protesting against
the Communist regime. Everything is symbolic in Poland and
every date is ingrained in the memory of each Polish soul, so
of course they would schedule the unveiling on a date which
would revere their patriots. "Along with wage demands and the
right to form free trade unions, the right to erect this memorial
was one of Solidarity's main demands during the 1980 lock-in.
The 42-metre, 139-ton steel sculpture stands on the spot where
the first three victims of the 1970 riots were killed. The three
crosses represent the three victims. At the top you see anchors
signifying the men's profession. The statue forms the centerpiece of what is known as Solidarity Square and surrounding
it are several memorials and plaques dedicated to victims of
totalitarianism."[10] A photograph of Pope John Paul II in bill-
board proportion dominates the entrance, while carved stone
tablets line the edge of the plaza along the fence line. The stark
simplicity of this massive memorial made me feel insignificant.

---

10 *In Your Pocket Essential City Guides – Gda sk: Monument of the Fallen
Shipyard Workers*

It's hard to fathom those oppressed shipyard workers having so much courage.

As we toured the museum, I found it incredible that their communications system, typewriters and simple news sources were so primitive and yet durable enough to accomplish what the world believed to be impossible. I kept thinking "What was it that swept over these people that would finally make them take matters into their own hands, without a gun, a tank, or a sword, and have the bravery to defy the Communists?" I remembered those days in our news media at home. It was the first time there had been daily news of Poland and these were the days that would change the world. At the end of the walk through museum tour there is a film which tells the story, describing the subsequent rolling strikes, imprisonments, and eventual freedom from Soviet domination, which further inspired other nation states to break loose from the empire which had suppressed them for so long.

Janet at shipyard

Mobs of people in the streets celebrated as each segment of the

Soviet bloc broke out of a symbolic brick wall and gained its freedom. The exhibit is named "Roads To Freedom." Lech Wałęsa and the Pope inspired the workers, the Poles, the people of the Soviet Union and the world.

As we were leaving the historic shipyard, I tried to buy a Solidarity flag that had flown over the famous gate #2. A man in the ticket booth kept telling Gosia I should buy a new flag which he had for sale. Translations went back and forth for several minutes before he relented and gave me one of the used flags. I tried to pay him for it but no, he wouldn't take my money for an old flag. My enthusiasm for an authentic flag which had flown over that historic site completely eluded him. It's one of my most treasured souvenirs from Poland. We made our way back to Gosia's flat in Warsaw where we rested and listened to Peter's imitations of Groucho Marx along with reciting favorite lines from gangster movies. Sometimes his jokes must be translated by Gosia. His enthusiasm is boundless, until Gosia's patience runs thin and he is banned to the balcony so that Gos can have some peace.

The car rental service sent a man with a Ford Focus in preparation for our trip south to Kolbuszowa. We all discussed paperwork and signing documents together. In Poland these things seem like a significant event. Everyone's attention is focused on the business at hand. Peter, taking responsibility for their recommendation, was attentive to each detail and safety issue. In the US, I would have treated such a matter very casually, assuming that all rental agencies are insured, cars in good working order, legal matters non-negotiable, and therefore sign the papers and get on the road as soon as possible.

However in Poland there is residue of old circumstances. People of a certain age can still remember when they had to be cautious about who they were dealing with and whether the arrangements would be fair. We take our laws and authorities for granted. Sometimes these lengthy discussions can be maddening because they use so many syllables to get the smallest piece of information – but it's the charm of their sincerity and caring that I love so much.

We packed the car and headed south wrestling with city streets and maps. Gosia would normally travel by taxi or train, not being a driver, so this escapade would require her to learn some new skills. I was confident that if she just read the signs to me we would be fine…and we were. Once away from the city, the two lane road passed many small settlements, farms, rows of poplar trees, and lots of new road construction. The shrines become more common as we move south. Each one is different. Some are small shelters the size of a bus stop, while others might be attached to a tree or a length of fencing. There are always bright colored artificial flowers and a cross or crucifix included. They are testimony to the intensity of the Polish faith. The shrines are more common in the south-east where my family originates in the hinterlands of Poland.

We decided to stop for a coffee break when we arrived in the charming old town of Sandomierz. The town was founded in 800 AD and you can still see structures that date to the early

1900s · · · · · 1920s · · · · · 1960s · · · · · 1970s · · · · · 1980s · · · · · 1990s

1200s. You could write a chapter on each of these short stops. Lace curtains in the summer breeze, window boxes filled with red geraniums, cafes with large umbrellas outside were all waiting for a festival being prepared in the square where they would be playing sea shanties.

Lovely as the little town was, we had a mission to complete and it was time to move further south to find our lodging for the night. "In the middle part of the River Vistula, in the heart of Poland, lies a gem of Polish architecture – the castle in Baranów Sandomierski. The former seat of the Leszczynski family, it is one of few well preserved magnate residences. Built in the late 16th and 17th centuries to a design by Santi Gucci, and modeled after Wawel castle in Kraków, surrounded by a breathtaking park, the castle fits perfectly into the landscape of the Vistula plains. The castle in Baranów is a three-floor building built on the plan of a rectangle. At its corners stand four round towers crowned with distinctive cupolas. The central part of the front façade comprises a protruding tower with the main entrance gate, leading through a stone portal into an enchanting arcaded courtyard."[11] We arrived at Baranów Castle which was perhaps a half hour shy of our destination of Kolbuszowa. This was the closest hotel Gosia could find where we could be certain of the accommodations. We didn't want another night like our first overnight in Kolbuszowa. At the reception desk they apologized that we couldn't be housed in the "new" building where

---

11 www.baranow.com.pl

business meetings take place, but rather we'd have to stay in a room at the castle itself. We came through the courtyard in awe of the architecture resembling the Wawel Castle's multiple arches, tiled roof, and stunning double staircase to the 2nd level balconies. When we opened the door to our room we were flabbergasted by the enormity of the room which was at least 30 feet long, the huge chandelier, Oriental rug, and massive furniture. Our casement windows opened to an English garden on one side and the spectacular court yard on the other. We sat under the arched and vaulted ceiling wondering how we deserved this castle living.

As we arrived in Kolbuszowa the next morning, we circled the town noting a recently constructed roundabout, numerous expensive automobiles and an increase in trade and activity since our last visit. Each time I've returned to Poland there is more and more prosperity evident as the empty shelves of the 70s morphed into major shopping malls in downtown Warsaw. Even the Skansen Village had grown as natives brought more buildings, farm implements, wind mill, farm animals and collections into the museum village. At Skansen's gift shop I found some Polish redware pottery, a small oil painting by a local artist, and a few hollyhock seeds from their gardens to bring home with me.

Discovering Grandfather's Church

We had learned from our research that grandfather's church had been moved about 7 kilometers away from Cmolas, so we followed directions to find the settlement called Poręby Dymarskie, where the church now resides. The country roads were small and barely paved as we travelled through fields, past shrines, clumps of woods and very few houses or other signs of life. Finally a clearing and still standing in all her glory is St. Stanislaus & St. Adalbert's Church, built in 1656-1660 and moved to Poręby Dymarskie from Cmolas in 1979.

Disassembled, relocated and restored by local farmers, it is used lovingly by the people of Poręby Dymarskie for their daily devotions. Circling around the exterior of the church on foot, I found it incredible that a group of non-professional moving men could have disassembled and then re-assembled this structure using such primitive tools, an ox and a cart! And yet there

2001 . . . . . . 2003 . . . . . 2006 . . . . .

it was, saved and cherished by the humble farmers of this tiny hamlet. We passed a young teen behind the church rehearsing a hymn for Sunday.

Inside, the hallway contained the rugged wooden poles used to hoist shrines during processions. As we entered the church proper, sun streamed through the windows illuminating the crimson rug and falling on the youngsters in the pews at summer bible camp. They gathered in this old church without fans or air conditioning to continue their studies in spite of the heat. This sort of devotion, consistent and unfailing is so much a part of the Polish nature. The young priest in black full length cassock spoke quietly to his students as he paced. The surrounding walls were covered with amazing early paintings uncovered when paneling was removed in preparation for its move from Cmolas. The altar is rich with old European gold. It was incredible richness in a quiet, confidant way, if that makes any sense. I felt I had arrived at an oasis in a desert. We knelt in a pew near the back so as not to interrupt the class and I felt the closeness to my grandparents' baptisms and their wedding in this very place. I'm still lost for words at the thought of it. The day was boiling hot yet these kids sat well behaved in their religious lessons from a priest whose collar and robes must have been stifling in the heat. I was barely conversational as I tried to internalize my find. There are times I hardly believe what I've done.

We searched Cmolas, questioning locals to try and find Witek's home and family. Foolishly I hadn't brought exact information with me. There is a man who travels to each house collecting for electric bills and he knew nothing about a family with this name. They must live in a different village. We had to abandon that search even though I knew it would be disappointing to Witek and his family.

Collecting our thoughts at lunch, Gosia reviewed the information we had pieced together so far. "Kolbuszowa was the administrative district in the 19th century. The administrative structure was and still is completely independent of the church divisions into parishes. I guess that explains the confusion about your folks saying they were from Kolbuszowa, because that was their administrative district created under the Austrians." Within the larger district there is a center known as Kolbuszowa as well the hamlets of Cmolas to the north, Zarębki in-between (Marcin's home) and Mechowiec northeast of Zarębki (where my grandmother Marianna came from). Cmolas is where St. Stanislaus & St. Adalbert's Church was located.

We learned that in August 1585 a 15 year old boy experienced a revelation and to this day his statue stands at the entrance to church grounds. When the boy grew to adulthood he painted the scene which he had witnessed and the painting remains in the modern church.

St. Stanislaus & St. Adalbert's Church was the parish church of Cmolas for many years, built in 1656-1660. It stood on a knoll surrounded by a masonry wall at a corner lot a few hundred yards from today's parish church.

In the 1960s the parish had a new church built, and for the next 15-20 years the old wooden church stood unused and deteriorating. The people of Poręby Dymarskie in the nearby settlement wished to have their own church and so there was an application to authorities to relocate the abandoned St. Stanislaus and St. Adalbert's church to their village. Twelve years later, permission to move the church was granted. The building was dismantled and reconstructed by local men, who found it necessary to replace the fabric of the entire tower as well as much of the exterior boards and the supports for the 'cupola'. In the process of dismantling the building they discovered the very early painting on the boards of the side walls within the presbytery – or as we refer to the area surrounding the altar in the U.S. – the sanctuary. When the authorities realized the old paintings existed, there was discussion about whether the move should be halted and the church would become a museum – but in the end the parishioners from Poręby Dymarskie prevailed.

There was also a smaller wood-frame church known as the "hospital" church built in the 1660s which was located in the same general area of Cmolas. We didn't understand the need for that 2nd church or why it was referred to as the "hospital" church. It was eventually moved to the walled lot at the corner where it stands today. It's a fascinating story to unravel about the churches being literally moved like checkers in and around Cmolas.

With all this moving and building of churches within such a tiny hamlet as Cmolas, it's small wonder we spent inordinate amounts of time attempting to follow the story. Each time we return to the subject, another piece of the puzzle reveals itself.

It seems you can never gather all the information on any subject at the same sitting. It takes time to cover several centuries of history as well as translating the culture of the situation. And so another segment of my search was completed with our visit to grandfather's church.

Grandfather's church

We headed back to our storybook castle passing many storks'
nests along the way. This is the area of Poland where there are
many of these majestic ivory birds who make their nests high
on poles.

We decided to stop in Sandomierz again on our journey
home. Gosia knew the story of Queen Jadwiga's white gloves
which were on display in a house museum there. Currently
owned by the Diocese, it is the charming brick and stone house
of Jan Długosz, built in 1416 and now used for travelling art
exhibits. The mercury had climbed and the low ceilings of this
non-air-conditioned building became oppressive to me, so I
sat near an open door at the vestibule. Gosia finished her tour
and joined me. Suddenly she alerted me to something she saw
behind me. She had spotted a simple black book at the ticket
desk with the words "Antoni Rząsa" on the cover. The cura-
tor priest sitting nearby came into our conversation to explain
that the display of religious wood carvings in the museum were
created by a man using an axe. The intricacy of the work is
astounding, considering his tools. We visited at precisely the
right time, just prior to the final day of the exhibit. The priest
explained that the artist was deceased but he started a "foundation" before he died where his son carries on his work today
and the son's name is, Marcin Rząsa! Amazement doesn't come
close to describing our feelings. After searching for the family
name for so long over many miles, it was astonishing to acci-
dentally find this Rząsa's work and then to learn his son has my
grandfather's exact name. All this on top of having just visited

my grandfather's church was nearly unbelievable to me.

Throughout the past few years prior to all of this, I continued to find bird's feathers at my feet when I got out of my car,
when entering certain buildings, or lying beside something I
was about to pick up. It happened often enough for me to ask
a Native American friend how her Indian lore would interpret
such an occurrence. "It's a message from the universe," she said.
"What's the message?!" Soon after finding several feathers in a
row I would discover a piece of information about grandfather
or make another trip to Poland. I've come to think the feathers
are symbolic of the pigeons grandfather housed in his backyard
at Derry Street.

As Gosia and I chattered about this latest Rząsa incident
while walking the sidewalk outside the little cottage, I looked
down...to find another feather at my feet. Gosia was beginning
to think there was something to all this feather folklore and we
chuckled at the fateful turns our search had taken.

Back in Warsaw we toured the gardens at the Palace of
Wilanów, visited with another Virtual Tourist pen pal, and for
August 1, we enjoyed the celebration of the Warsaw Uprising.
The ceremony was filled with uniforms, flags, music, flowers
and live TV coverage. This was a big day for these people who
had suppressed the story of their brave patriots for so many
years. There were a few men brought from other countries who
had been part of the Uprising and they were proud to don their
old uniforms and berets and speak that day. I learned that the
Boy Scouts marched in the procession, since they had acted as

messengers during the uprising, a number of them having lost their lives.

We had lunch at the Blikle Café, in existence since 1869 and popular with many notables before the war. It served as a canteen for the fighting men during the Uprising. It was bombed and levelled along with the rest of Warsaw but as is common here, they rebuilt it exactly as it was before the bombs fell. Restored to the art deco design, reminiscent of the war years, it is finished with dark wood, Bentwood chairs, deco lights and American war year's music playing. "You must remember this; a kiss is still a kiss," I sang softly with the music and caught a Polish woman across the room smiling at the singing, American, visitor to her city.

Returning from another trip to Poland, I bubbled over, telling the stories of our homeland – but it isn't real to family and friends. I guess it is common that one person becomes possessed with the genealogy of a family and takes the responsibility of documenting its history, while others struggle to follow what you describe.

Władek Joins
the Search

In October I found another kindred spirit who shared a passion for this kind of documentation. By this time I had received emails from many other seekers who had found my postings on VirtualTourist and Ancestry.com. When this email arrived, I knew I had made another very special connection.

"Hallo Janet

The first what should I do it was introduced to you. You know my name...Władysław Rząsa. I'm 25 years old. I've back from UK and have moved to Kraków so I'm not living in Poręby Dymarskie but every second week I'm going back to my really home which is still there. I didn't even ask you how should I call you? Is Janet OK?

Lets back to the main topic. I've found your web site on yahoo. You know.That my passion..founding the informations about my village. I know almost everything but I want more and more so I'm looking for even in English web site.

About my surname…also yours grandfather surname…Rząsa (do you know how to read that surname…I know it's very hard…especially that the first A is the letter which you haven't got in your alphabet. This A we read like= ON)

But that is not the most important informations

I know that all RZĄSA came from Poręby Dymarskie. (that my g.fathers words!) My village is not a typical village like you think. There is 18 parts (smaller villages) with different names. I'm living in part which we call Dziuby (that also polish surname. There is only 6 farms, around fields and big forest) but your grandfather came from Wielkie Pole (Big or Great Field). Ages before on that area which we call Big Field was only few houses, farms. One of that was my great grandfathers farm and on that time that area people had called RZĄSOWKA (land of family Rząsa or Rząsa House). It means that Rząsa have been living there many generations. I know the informations only to great grandfaather so it hard to say something about the connections. I will check that for you. My g.dad don't know too much. He forgot everything. It was very hurt for us. He had brother Joseph Rząsa. After II World War he left Poland and spent all life in Chicago. We dont know nothing about him. Probably he's dead because he was the oldest…but my grandfather's sister has good health and remembers so I will ask my dad to talk with her.

My great g.father dead in 1953 so he was born about 1880? If we are related we need to found my great g.father's name and the names of his brothers…

It's funny to talk about being related..so many generations, but I understand that is important for you, that somewhere is somebody who could be my family, that I'm not alone, are really nice.

I will try to help you.

What you think about my English…I know it's no perfect but I'm hope is not so bad.

I didn't know that you was Rząsa before married…I'm really surprise of that situations…I only wanted try maybe somebody want to write something about my village?

It is real life…You never know what happen to you.

You can write as much as you want, but give me a time for answer.

I enclose my photo.

Władek (that a short version of Władysław)"

The men who moved the church;
Photo from Władek Rząsa's collection

Messages flew back and forth in the following days as we acquainted ourselves with one another's knowledge of

Kolbuszowa, Cmolas, and the very special church. Władek was a Rząsa living in Poręby Dymarskie and a communicant of St. Stanislaus and St. Adalbert's parish. What a stroke of luck this new connection was. The odds of this are rare. We joked that we would someday find a family connection, but I knew it had to be with the name being so unique to his small region in Poland. Władek knew the men who moved the church and in fact, his grandfather was one of them. Photos of the dozen or so men in simple working clothes standing by the massive beams were sent over the internet along with a picture of my new pen pal. So unusual to find such a young man spending time with researching the history of his village as well as someone else's family and I treasured his attention. He and a friend created a web site for Poręby Dymarskie and he asked me to write the story of my search for family to be posted there. Gosia's brilliant translation skills kicked in again and the story was posted in Polish.

Władek brought his father into our relentless searching as they went to House #60 in Zarębki and knocked on the door. No one answered but when questioning neighbors, they discovered that the Rząsa family no longer owned the house. It wouldn't be unusual to find descendants still living on the land in this village that barely keeps step with the modern world. They did come away with more photos of the land and street which clarified my imagination of grandfather's life. Władek wrote, "You know the place. I will try to find for you actual map that you will have same to locate that place when you come to Poland. I sure that you will do it."

He visited the town archives and sent copies of the old maps to show exactly where grandfather's house stood. Their version of our plat maps look like narrow strips of land arcing across the landscape. Their numbering system isn't revised as the area is subdivided and settled, so the lot numbers are not in succession. We see numbers 31, 33, 2, 29, 9, 11 and so on with small rectangular blocks representing houses at the road's edge and long strips of farm-able land behind each house. Władek was right. I wanted to go and see that exact place.

Land lots in Kolbuszowa

I found an address to write to Antoni Rząsa's family, the artist we discovered in Sandomierz. I was fascinated that I had located another Marcin Rząsa, Antoni's son, who had obviously created a web site. His wife, Magda answered my email.

2001 · · · · · 2003 · · · · · 2006 · · · · 2008 · · · ·

"Hello Janet, Antoni Rząsa was born in Futoma, powiat Blazowa near from Rzeszow in this village there is a lot of families Rząsa. We don't know anything about cousins from Kolbuszowa. I think the family can be very very big, because it was a tradition to have lot of children (Antoni had 5 brothers and sisters...) in all generations. It seems to be very difficult to build a complete genealogic tree...In our house in Zakopane, which was built by Antoni Rząsa we have a Museum of Rząsa's sculptures. We organize also a lot of expositions out of Zakopane. Marcin is also sculpture. So he divide his time and energy between Promotion of his father and his own work. Greetings, Magda."

I found photographs of Marcin's carving and knew it was only a matter of time before I would plan another trip to find the artist in Zakopane, as well as the little plot of land where grandfather lived.

Trying to understand the motivation of my grandfather to take on the perilous journey to the United States, I searched for everything I could find written about the period of time between Marcin's birth in Poland and the time he left. Without personal accounts, I relied on the work of researchers and historians, or writers from other families who could report on the Kolbuszowa district's economic, political and social conditions during that period.

Just prior to my grandfather's birth the abolition of serfdom in 1848 brought about a process of social and political change.[12]

---

12 Serf: A person in feudal servitude, attached to the lord's land and transferrable with it from one owner to another.

Kealy Stouter-Halsted writes, "Serfdom eroded only very slowly, and the social distance peasants felt from their farmer landlord remained wide." There was the "pressure of land shortages, a growing rural population, primitive farming techniques, persistent and pre-harvest famine, intermittent epidemics, and almost complete absence of correctives available to help the peasants out of their immiserated situation. Since Galician peasants at mid-century lived very close to the margins of survival, among the immediate concerns that would form the core of their political agenda were issues related to subsistence."

Around the time of grandfather's birth, the villages of the Galician district were still experiencing the growing pains which emancipation had brought. Having been released from serfdom, the local governments which were created had many problems in the process of learning the business of self-government. The continued separation of gentry from peasants meant the community was forced to struggle with the responsibility of road work, schools, hospitals and taxation within their communes.

The chaos of local administration, the ravages of alcoholism, high death rates, and widespread peasant dependence on usury were reported in statistical studies of the period. The state of the Galician countryside in the early 1880s was that almost half of all Galician villages had no school and that over 80% of village mayors could neither read nor write. Researchers reported that Galician peasants were unable to attend school in winter for lack of shoes to wear.

Thirty years after emancipation, rural economic and cultural conditions showed little improvement over those of pre-emancipation. These were the conditions which Marcin, my grandfather, was born into and the environment he grew up in until he was required to serve in the Austrian Army and then ultimately left Poland in 1905.

I read with personal interest what Keeley Stouter-Halsted wrote in *The Nation In The Village* about the young men (including Marcin Rząsa) being inducted into the Austrian Army in the late 1800s. "Military recruits and their leave taking became an important part of the village calendar. In October there were all night festivities before their departure. Villagers marched behind the recruits in a hierarchy reflecting their relationship to the recruits. Hired musicians walked with them to the edge of the village where the recruits climbed into waiting wagons and physically separated themselves from the village of their birth and from their weeping families."

In "foreign" places the recruits often feared their own officers more than enemy bullets. There were nasty German officers and German doctors. Villagers expanded their horizons with stories from returning soldiers of far off lands visited: Italy, Bosnia, France, Prussia, Rome and Berlin. I longed to know about grandfather's experience in the army, but these general descriptions of conditions at that time were all that I had.

Another of my sources reported "Galicia, the largest province of the Austrian Empire still paid the highest rate of income taxes in Europe and as a result, two million people emigrated

from Galicia by 1914, mostly to the United States. Mass starvation reached catastrophic proportions claiming up to 50,000
dead during the worst years. The losses would have been greater
if emigration had not occurred." Clearly, this would contribute
to why my grandfather decided to leave his homeland, no matter how difficult it would be for him or his wife.

Reading these works brought to mind my third journey home
from Poland when I was seated next to Witek on the plane. His
life consisted of working for a large contractor painting synagogues in Brooklyn during the winter months, and returning
to Poland for the summer. It was the way he earned enough
money to build a modern house and save for his daughters'
future education in America. As he talked about his migratory
life, I realized this was the explanation for the neighborhoods I
had seen around Cmolas. Although there was no visible means
of livelihood in this tiny remote village, there were sections of
newly constructed sizeable homes scattered throughout the tiny
streets. I had asked Gosia repeatedly how it was possible for all
of this to exist. The Brooklyn connection explained it.

When my grandfather left Poland to seek a better life for
himself and his family, there were several brothers left behind.
Whatever land holdings there were could not support the families of each brother. In such a Catholic environment you would
expect that each son would marry and produce several children.
And so, between my visits to the Skansen village and the volumes of research I had poured through, I came to understand
the condition of Cmolas and Kolbuszowa as my ancestors grew

into adulthood. Still one link was missing in the puzzle of the immigration story. Where did the money come from to make such a trip?

On a Sunday in March, 2008 I wrote in my journal:

"I've been thinking about Uncle Mike and Aunt Jenny a lot lately. Sometimes I wake up with them on my mind. Last week's call and message went unanswered, so I called this morning. The answering machine picked up, but I left no message. I wondered if they could be out at church. I hoped nothing dreadful had happened to them. Their kids had never been friendly and, in fact, had never spoken to me at funerals or any time I went for a visit. I worry they wouldn't call me if my uncle were really sick or if Mike or Jenny died. I wonder if they avoid everyone in the Zosa family because of stories they've heard from their parents about the troubled times of my Aunt Agnes' kids. They used to say, 'you could never let those people in your house. They can't be trusted. They would steal and lie.' I hope my aunt was clear about which cousins had the bad reputations, but I sense her children may have been warned to keep their mouths shut and stay clear of the entire family.

Well, I couldn't let the day go by without another try at calling this last sibling of my mother's. I had to know they were O.K.

On the next call Aunt Jenny answered the phone. She was pleasant and chatty – apologizing for not calling me back last week. She said her son in law had been in and out of the hospital with a heart problem and Uncle Mike's legs were really giving him trouble. I told her I was worried about them and would like to visit but she said, 'It's like a mad house around here. I'd like to see you, but maybe another time. This really isn't a good time.' I asked her to please say hello to my Uncle Mike and tell him I hope he feels better soon. There was no more to say. We have no relationship to discuss. I tried to mention a few things about us but she was clearly interested in getting finished with our telephone conversation, and so I let her go. I thought I felt that thump again. It always comes at the end of my conversations with members of the Zosa family. It's like a door slams shut and I feel as if I've been told to keep my nose out of there.

I wondered if she was protecting Michael from another round of discussions about his mother. Maybe my visits open too many old wounds. I know my relentless digging into the past is difficult for some people, but I cannot stop without uncovering the entire story. Although our conversation was civil, I had an awful feeling when I got off the phone. The last of my mother's siblings, the only direct link to my grandfather was unavailable to me. Maybe I read too much into it but I don't think so. My only hope is that it was a bad day for me to call and I might have better luck at another time."

Władek's emails continued and I was grateful to have his help with researching the family records. He had moved to London for work and travelled home to Poręby Dymarskie as often as he could. I think it was hard for him to separate himself from his homeland, and it made me think of the similarities among my grandparents, Witek, Władek and so many other Poles who were forced to emigrate for work.

His accommodation in answering so many questions was very valuable to me since his experience and that of the people he knew in the Kolbuszowa district gave me more specific details of the life my grandfather had lived. I had read about the lack of schools, education, and the shoes to walk to school in Halstead's[13] accounts and so I asked what Władek knew about all this.

> "I got access to the web site where all old doc and there is a list of elementary schools in each village and the name of the teacher. Kolbuszowa had in1800s a good school and even secondary school. I'm 100% that secondary (male and female) school was in Kolbuszowa in the earliest 1900s. In other villages as [in mine] a small school with one or two classes. In Por by Dymarskie first school started in 1910, but before this time we had a teacher who was walking from house to house and he was teaching children. I think it was the same in Zar bki, so your grandfather should have some education. [Count] Tyszkiewicz (land lord of Kolbuszowa) was a good man so he care about education, but people on this time wasn't. My great grandfather finished 6 classes of school. My grandfather also, but his wife had only 3 classes because of IIWW. My father couldn't go to secondary school because my grandparents didn't want him to taste a life in town. But he went to work and there meet my mum who also had been told by parents to not go to school. She really wanted but they wanted all children working for themself so she started work in the factory at 14 years old as my father.
>
> About the other things, I will be in Poland when you will come to Kolbuszowa for one week so I will help you translate everything."

---

13 Kelly Stouter Halstead, *The Nation in the Village: The Genesis of Peasant National Identity in Austrian Poland 1848–1914*

(1900s) · · · · · (1920s) · · · · · (1960s) · · · · · (1970s) · · · · · (1980s) · · · · · (1990s)

Władek continued to visit the Family History Center where he culled many files of Rząsa births and baptisms as he tried to hypothesize relationships within the tree. It was dizzying to follow who was the wife, son, or illegitimate child with repeating names and odd spellings which continue to confuse me. The most important record he found was Marcin's New York passenger arrival at Ellis Island on April 7, 1905 giving his last residence as "Za...abka." This listing gave his departure port as Hamburg, marital status as married, and arrival age at 37 years. Again I doubted the validity of this document; his given age didn't make sense.

We concluded that our vertical search for the family line needed to shift. What we needed were Marcin's siblings to determine the interrelationships of the Rząsa members. The proper ship arrival information would eventually surface especially for grandmother and Peter's arrival. (All of this part of the search might have been avoided if Uncle Peter had allowed access to the papers and documents which he claimed to dispose of after his parents' deaths).

As the months and years moved along, my websites brought more people trying to connect and share their information. Each of us has a portion of the greater family tree, and one day I hope we can connect all the fragments. I've heard from Rząsa clan from Australia to Connecticut and across the globe to Poland. Sometimes the coincidences are amazing. One woman, Rose, wrote to say her grandfather was also from Kolbuszowa. I asked where she was writing from, and it turns out she lives less

than 5 miles from my home. We later discovered from old property maps, that the two grandfathers lived 3 or 4 lots away from
one another in that little remote village of my grandfather's
birth. Our meeting and search seemed fated. Rose was active
with Ancestry and was excited about finding all the information
uncovered by Władek. When it came time to plan the next trip,
she and her sister would join Gosia and me in Kraków and then
Kolbuszowa. She needed to locate the church and records of her
family which could be done only by visiting in person as was
true for me. There was no prediction as to when the records of
Kolbuszowa would eventually be digitized, if ever.

Fifth Trip
to Poland

Krakow

Zakopane

Kolbuszowa

Cmolas

Zarębki

Poręby Dymarskie

On my next trip I flew directly to Kraków, placing me closer to Kolbuszowa rather than spending time travelling south from Warsaw. My hotel sent a driver to the airport to collect me and once settled, it was a short walk to the square. I was feeling familiar as I went to lunch in a favorite café and shopped for a few groceries in a small market close by. Gosia wouldn't hear

of me travelling unescorted, so she took the train from Warsaw to join me. How bizarre to feel so relaxed that day as if
meeting Gos for coffee in Kraków was commonplace. We were
old friends and accustomed to living and travelling together in
many cities.

Zakopane Artist

First on our agenda was to find the Rząsa studio owned by
the artist we had discovered in Sandomierz on the last trip.
Gosia had not been to Zakopane since she was very young, so
we were both looking forward to the adventure. There is a 2½
hour bus ride to climb to Zakopane. Once there, you walk ten
minutes to the main street which runs up hill and is lined with
restaurants and local souvenir stands. Zakopane has for a century played the role of Poland's winter capitol, not only because
of its advantages for tourism and sport, but because it has been a
favorite haunt of intellectuals, musicians, painters, and writers.
The wooden churches and cottages are masterpieces of these
unrivalled highland carpenters. Here in the Tatra Mountains
the traditions, native costumes, and foods are as unique to this
region as their architecture.

We discovered that Rząsa didn't have a gallery on the main
street but at an address some distance from the center. We hired
a cab to find it. When we arrived we had the feeling the gallery was not open to the public. The driver pulled into what

looked like someone's back yard, but there was a sign, so we decided to ring the bell. A handsome curly haired man came to the door and invited us into the gallery. I immediately saw my favorite piece which had been exhibited in Sandomierz a few years ago. Gos translated that the piece was a favorite of both artists: Antoni and Marcin. It was done by Antoni when he was about 43 or 44 years old before Marcin was born. The story goes that when Antoni returned from a trip to Rome he was very depressed. He told his family and friends, "Everything has been done." He couldn't work for six months, but then he created perhaps his greatest work (and my favorite) St. Francis. Marcin was born when Antoni was 46 and growing up, Marcin felt as if the piece was his "older brother."

The studio holds numerous sculptures created by Antoni Rzasa – the father of the man who greeted us. It is interesting to see the framed pieces which accompany the sculptures showing the artist's first sketches of his intended work. Sometimes it is a quick idea dashed on the back of an envelope which later becomes a piece of wonderful sculpture in fruitwood. It was amazing to think that Antoni worked with an axe.

Marcin spoke in Polish to Gosia and eventually beckoned his wife, Magda (who speaks English), their son and daughter to join us, and we were invited into their personal space for tea. Photos of Antoni and Marcin are scattered around the house and studio, the wife of Antoni being an adept photographer. Marcin's wife serves as the promoter, and teaches at the local art school as well as being mother and homemaker. The father's work is not for sale — and will not be sold, but is exhibited in many places around Poland, France, and an upcoming trip to Italy. Marcin and Magda planned to retrace his father's steps.

Marcin's son seems very close to his daddy and Marcin is obviously a sensitive and loving father. His work shows that sensitivity to his children. They brought us into Marcin's studio where all his wood sculptures were scattered. I went straight to the very favorite among his pieces, an angel seated on a chair. "Well that is not for sale," Gosia translated. Next I chose a few of his figures of little girls and

Marcin Rząsa and his family at his studio in Zakopane... the artist with my grandfather's name – his father, Antoni's sculpture in rear.

again, "that is a favorite and not for sale." And so it went until I finally pleaded for him to duplicate one of the favorites. He was reluctant to do the same thing twice, warning that no two can ever be exactly the same. He hesitates to sell any of his work, like his father, and he's obviously attached to his angel and the children he's carved on a far smaller scale than the senior Rząsa's work. He agreed he would try to create another pig-tailed girl. Arrangements could be made to send it down the mountain to Kraków with the local bus driver before I left for home. In Zakopane it is evidently common for the bus driver to carry things for locals in order to save the 2.5 hour drive into the city. I photographed the family in the gallery with the big German shepherd family dog all standing in front of Marcin's "older brother." It was more meaningful to see the work in this place where you had a strong feeling of the artist in his own space. Antoni built the house where Marcin and his family now live, and Marcin continues to carve.

Unfortunately they knew very little about Marcin's heritage except to know the family was from the Rzeszów area. Magda thought it would be very difficult to create a tree to include so many children in each generation. I was disappointed that we couldn't gather more family information, but enchanted with having met this family of artists, whom I knew in my heart, was part of my clan.

We left waving and thanking them over and over. Marcin walked outside to say goodbye and watch us leave – his charming dimples flashing and his silvered curls shining in the afternoon sun.

Continuous Immersion

Back in Kraków we travelled in the steps of Pope John Paul II, to St. Anna's where he prayed across from the Jagiellonian University, where he studied. We found there are commemorative coins to collect from each of the churches he was connected to, and we started a collection for a friend at home. Next we visited St. Adalbert's, then St. Mary's and finally a visit to the Apostles' Church. As I turned to leave the foyer of one of the churches, there inside the building lay a bird's feather at my feet. By now even Gosia was beginning to think there was something to all this feather business.

Władek, Gosia and Janet

Rose and her sister arrived and settled in Kraków, and I rented a car to drive to Kolbuszowa. When we arrived at the Skansen village where Władek's father had arranged our lodging, there was a festival in progress with hundreds of people enjoying the costumed dancers, singers, and colorful stands selling homemade baked goods, pierogi and beer. Władek found us in spite of the crowd. I'm sure being Americans we stuck out like sore thumbs. Władek was joined by his sister and parents to meet us and invite us to their home the next day. I was delighted to accept their kind invitation and honored they had taken the afternoon to come into town to greet us. We enjoyed the festival and village, sat comparing notes, discussing our family tree, and generally getting to know one another. Władek and his sister led us (on her scooter) to gather groceries for our stay here, and we settled into the modest but clean guest rooms on the second floor of the Skansen Village reception building.

Waking up in Skansen Village was such a treat with green fields, a small lake and vast blue sky outside my window. I stared at the scene, trying to commit it to my memory forever, while the rest of them slept. I was so thankful to be in this special place. We connected with Władek and drove to see the old priest in Cmolas. The morning developed into confusion when the senior priest arrived and tried to stop our search. Gosia persisted that we would have our information. The priest insisted that a Personal Data Privacy Act prohibited them from opening the books. His argument increased in speed and volume as we all watched. I didn't need the language to know that Gos was countering every point; she had no intention of retreating. She finished with a slight smile and a back handed compliment about the Catholic Church always in search of truth. He finally softened, perhaps realizing he had met his match. She wasn't afraid of him like his parishioners. The sweet older priest, poor soul, head lowered, was covering his eyes as if he could hardly bear to hear the ranting of his superior another moment.

Once Gosia had convinced the head priest that we should be given the information we sought, there was the question of how best to obtain the data, given the design and format of how the books were kept. There was no index, but the books were separated by village. Within each book, notations of births were made by date, with quite a wide range in each book. The head priest suggested we begin with my grandfather's parents' wedding date and move forward. Because children were born at home and families stayed in the same house for generations, Władek suggested it would be faster to scan the column which listed the house numbers. This way we could discover all the children born of my great grandparents – providing me with a list of grandfather's siblings. Along the way we also discovered that numerous Skowron babies were also born in that same house; #60 in Zarębki. We followed the process to the end of the book until the birth of Marcin was found. Władek assumes he was the youngest in the family, however Władek and the priest did not continue beyond his birth to verify that.

In the end I had gained information about all 6 siblings and a few of the Skowrons. What a great morning! This meant that I could now begin to connect to others who had contacted me about their Rząsa family members. I now had this horizontal group who might be ancestors to others who knew only their vertical line of ancestry. I made arrangements to have a mass said for Marcin Rząsa and family and offered several tokens from America to the priest. He said he would pass them along to his pastor, which of course wasn't what I wanted, but it was his humble, subservient way.

Father Józef Zóttek

We drove several miles through pine and birch forests and open fields of oats until we reached Władek's family farm in Poręby Dymarskie. The air was flawless, and the blue sky came down to meet the horizon creating a pure and peaceful scene. Władek's parents, brother and future sister- in-law were all on hand to greet us. Opening their simple home with pride, Władek told us of all that his father had built or created. They live off the land in true farm style. "My parents don't buy any-thing but salt and pepper," Władek quipped. It may not be that extreme but they certainly live independently within their fields and in sync with nature. Władek's mum prepared her white (sour rye) Borsch and they taught us to eat it the real Polish way with a spoon of melted lard in it. We were doubtful, but it was delicious. Władek's father supplied us with his homemade kielbasa, and we ripped pieces of whole rye bread made by mama. She also made the butter which was a flawless oval yellow mound as nicely presented as those perfectly shaped little bits served in fine restaurants. There were small wooden stools to seat everyone at the table in the room that doubled for a living room. Photo albums came out so we could see the family from childhood, the parents' marriage, and the photos of the church being re-built after its move.

I asked Władek's father to show me his farm. We saw the bull and two cows in the small barn – a horse and three month old pony in another small space. Władek had us skip the pigs, "They stink! We'll smell like pigs when we go to the next church." The old hay barn also housed straw. It had been repaired over the years but was the same barn used for generations. None of the structures were very big. Chickens ran in the yard with assorted cats and a couple of dogs. We examined the mounded hole for potatoes (cold storage) with a canvas flap for a door. The vegetable garden was tended by the small dog who kept out rabbits and such. When I said the squirrel had dug Hoot's onions at home, they didn't believe it was a squirrel and father went to get a rather substantial sling shot to give me ideas for my husband. We chuckled. There was a lot of triple kissing as we left, and I had Władek translate that I was grateful to his father for letting me see how my grandfather lived on the farm. Władek translated back, "The barn would be the same as your grandfather's but the house would be wood with thatched roof like the Skansen village." Photos, waves, kisses and hugs followed and I thought, "What sweet people with such big open welcoming hearts."

Gosia and I had quite a laugh as we were driving the narrow country road through the farmland on our way back to Skansen. Gos' cell phone rang and she seemed startled when she answered. The man's unrecognizable voice said in Polish, "Hello, this is Marcin Rząsa." Gos had to process that thought for a moment. "Wait a minute. Janet's grandfather is dead! ... Oh, yes, it's the artist." We made jokes about "Oh, now I have to channel her grandfather through my cell phone! Her and her damned feathers!" The feathers continue to appear, by the way. Everyone laughs and probably thinks I'm a foolish woman, but each time I find another, I am reminded of my grandfather and soon after there is another reference to him or something is discovered about my family.

The following days were spent visiting churches to complete the sisters' research on their family but Władek and I managed to slip away to Zarębki while the rest of the women explored a local fair. We found #60 where so many Rząsa and Skowron family members had been born. Władek knocked at the door of the simple house, obviously newer than the original Rząsa home. The woman who answered knew nothing about the earlier owners of the property. As the Polish conversation proceeded, I busied myself taking pictures of the many pigeons on her roof — obvious descendants of my grandfather's pigeons. We crossed the street and knocked on other doors until we came to Ms. Kapusta, an older woman, who came out of the barn wearing an apron and babushka. She remembered many of the earlier neighbors. She spoke of three sisters who came from Poręby Dymarskie to marry three men from the Rząsa and Kapusta families. This was a link between Władek's village people and my ancestry. She also remembered Wiktoria (Polish for Victoria) Rząsa, who wasn't very well liked. Władek and I chuckled to think that Wiktoria's reputation was the same here as in my grandfather's experience. Ms. Kapusta said Wiktoria eventually married and moved to the States in the 1960s. She was the last

Janet and Lady Kapusta

of the Rząsa family to live on this street in Zarębki. Others left for Brooklyn, one to become a baker and another, a priest.

Before leaving I photographed the storks living high on a pole in a huge sloppy nest. There are more storks in this southeast area of Poland than anywhere else in the world. They are magnificent creatures.

We returned to Kraków, the sisters left for home, and Gosia

and I were able to meet with Magda who had come down from Zakopane to deliver the little girl sculpture Marcin had carved for me. We met for another lingering visit over coffee and I received my treasure created by the man with my grandfather's name…a true Polish naïve wood sculpture. These days, people, and occurrences just knock me out.

I dashed off an email to Władek as soon as I got home to thank him and his family for a wonderful visit. He replied,

"Halo Janet – I'm really glad to hear you. I can say that I miss you all. You were a great company for me. Your friends were lovely. I never met such a great "strangers" and feel so good with them. I wish that someday we will spend more time together and it will not be so crazy. Before I went to Poland to see you I put some purposes and the main one was to let you know Poland better, and explain you more about our region. I know I didn't say all I wanted. I didn't even show you everything. I think I will leave that for next journey. My parents also enjoyed your visit, and I'm also happy that you meet them. I think you will understand me more. You can't even imagine how hard for me it's leaving my family and my village. I think you had this same feelings when you were leaving Poland first time. My English friends are asking me about you every day. They also were keeping fingers crossed for our searching. I need to finish now. Say hallo to Rose and Czesla. Say big thank you to Gosia for helping us. And the last thing send me your address so I will send you my photos. Have a nice day, Your polish cousin, Władek"

There it was – another prediction of my next visit to Poland. There must be magic to their words because it gets in my head and haunts me until the next trip is planned.

More and more and more...

I was excited to report my latest findings to Uncle Michael and didn't know when I would be able to visit so I sent a letter describing some of my days in Poland.

"On this trip I met a young man I have been emailing for more than three years. He's a Rząsa and has been helping me with family research. I was thrilled to visit his family's farm on this visit. The farm was very similar to the place where your father grew up. I also saw the land where Martin was born and lived. We spoke to neighbors and discovered that Wiktoria lived across the street and was part of a branch of the Rząsa family. Evidently no one in Poland liked Wiktoria any more than Martin did! We laughed over that.

"My visit to the church and the old priest brought much more information about the family. I now have the names of all of your father's siblings. This will enable me to connect to other Rząsa families who have been researching their Polish roots. I'd also like to connect to the Skowrons. You remember it was Agnes Skowron who sponsored Martin when he came to the US.

"I arranged for two masses to be said in Poland for Marcin Rząsa and his family. One would be in the church where he was baptized and married in Poręby Dymarskie on July 12 and the other in the Cmolas church where I found all the records of the family on July 22. Władek's parents promised to attend the Poręby Dymarskie mass for us on July 12. I hope we would all be together in thought and prayer on that day."

In the following weeks, Władek and I exchanged emails and

photos taken in Poland as well as new versions of our family tree. It became confusing because of so many Marias, Mariannas, Magdalenas and Józefs. There was another more important point of confusion which Władek clarified. "You will see that in your family many times people were married in this same family. It's nothing wrong. That was a tradition. Ages ago the church promoted that kind of marriages because people didn't have to split land. You can also see that Jan Skowron married Marianna Pyra and Wojciech Pyra married John Skowron sister. Their parents didn't have to give them any land and that was good for both family." In other words, marrying cousins within the family was common and practical. Creating a family tree in this case is a real challenge. It isn't unique to my family but this practice hadn't occurred to me in trying to sort out relationships. As you insert the information into the traditional Ancestry.com tree, the system isn't set up to accommodate such oddities in today's world. Knowing all this enabled us to position the names properly, but not without a challenge. Władek plowed through while patiently explaining to me over and over again.

On a Sunday in September of 2010 I felt I had to visit my Uncle Michael and bring the Kolbuszowa Anniversary book to him. I was really nervous about the kind of reception I might get after being discouraged to visit the last time I called. I feared they might be in a nursing home or worse. Michael was now 89 years old.

I moved cautiously and as I opened the sun porch door, I was as surprised as Uncle Michael. He sat on the porch working on a

jig saw puzzle. I hugged him and he was quick to tell me there
was bad news about Aunt Jenny. She had cancer and had been
suffering about a year. I could see her depleted body in the living room as she napped under a blanket. I told him some of my
stories and most especially that he had an Uncle Michael. He
seemed astonished but intrigued and happy. I gave him photos
of the church which he seemed genuinely pleased with. When
I showed him the photos of Władek and his father, telling him
the father looked familiar to me, he said, "He's the spitting
image of my father!" I was shocked at that. His memory of his
father would be when he was much younger. I've never even
seen a photo of my grandparents when they were young. He said
he had received my mail. It made me glad that he had it clearly
in his mind. He was alert and said he felt good. The visit was
brief because he needed to tend to Aunt Jenny. I hope I brightened his day and gave him some respite from his obvious worry.

Władek continued to educate me on the local history of our
shared community. There were many emails explaining local
customs and the way the villages developed within Kolbuszowa.

> "In the fields now you can find many iron ores and that was a
> reason those villages were built. In my village there were two
> blacksmiths' factories. One called Rude (which means iron
> ore) the other Dymarka (furnace). In the 1500s they were the

property of the Mielecki family and were a part of Cmolas. Mechowiec (bellows) and Zarębki (in that time was called Dubas which means a little oak boat) were also located in Cmolas. Zarębki mined the iron ore from their fields and send them to my village by boat to melt and do iron. People in Mechowiec were working there as well. I think that iron from my village was used to build the Palace in Baranów Sandomierski. Legend says that the king's son or some prince came to that area for hunting and was killed by a bear. Because they couldn't find the body they started cutting the primeval forest, discovered iron ore, and that is how Dymarka developed."

Władek's capacity for probing the old records was relentless. He found evidence of the three women from his neighborhood who married three men who lived on my grandfather's street. That came from the lead Ms. Kapusta gave us on my last visit to Poland. The men they married were Rząsa and Kapusta. The much disliked Wiktoria was descended from this Rząsa union. That was the last of the Rząsa family to live on grandfather's street in Zarębki.

Władek found the twisted scenario of a brother and sister marrying another brother and sister whose grandchildren were my grandparents. He has the ability to sort out the relationships among many records with repetitive names and make sense of it all.

He gave me a typed list of every name on grandfather's street as of 1850 and beyond. All of this requires many hours of transcribing very old records and maps which are handwritten and would be hard to decipher if they were in English – never mind the Polish spellings with so many consonants, I would never be sure of the proper spelling. The more I learned, the more Polish I felt. I had come to understand so much more about life in Poland and my grandfather.

As my birthday rolled around, Władek wrote to say he was working on my gift which would be a little late. We were both delighted with the results of this latest discovery.

> "I know how much that all means to you that is also a reason why I spent so much time doing it. The records which you received are from Mormons – Family History Centre. I ordered films from Cmolas parish and spent hours looking at them in London. I find out the connection between your family and people who were living in my farm by accident because I always wanted to know about them. You wondering why? It easy answer. My great grandmother inherited all of it after her first husband death. I will send you more info about my farm, where was the old house, etc. but after Easter. One more thing I wanted to say to you. I didn't know my grandmother step-brother because he died in 1985. I saw somewhere some of his photos and I remember his hair was completely grey as yours and there was some similarity of you two. Maybe someday I will find that picture in my grandma other brother family. I think that will be enough for today and I will answer all your questions after Easter. Yours – W"

His gift was the family tree of both his family and mine connecting through his great grandmother. He had completed my grandmother's ancestry which went back to my great, great grandfather who lived at #35 in Poręby Dymarskie! "That is my family's address!" he gasped – amazed at his own discovery. Finally there was a connection between our families and although it was through a second marriage and very distant, we've chosen to call ourselves "cousins."

The coincidences continue.... and yes, I believe there are guardians or angels guiding my path through Poland.

April 22, 2011, Good Friday, I was discussing my "connections" with a friend as we sat in a cafe in my home town. On the way home, I thought about a customer who had so many wonderful Easter bunnies displayed in his home. It made me want more bunnies. I noticed that Claire's antique shop on the hill was still open so I swung in. I told her I was looking for a bunny.

"I just moved one the other day. It was hidden in the bottom of that case and I thought I should bring it out where it could be seen for Easter. It's around here somewhere. I've forgotten where I put it." Her shop is packed tightly with dishware, glassware, figurines, costume jewelry, and of course, the dozens of collectible tea cups that Gosia was enamored of when she was here. We both wandered around the three rooms of the shop until I spotted an absolutely perfect bunny on a shelf where even she was surprised that she had placed it. He was fabulous! She said the piece was a nice collectible. "You must know this name. It's Cybis – from Warsaw, Poland." I had never heard of these porcelain pieces, but I was astounded that it would be from Poland which meant that of course I would have to own it. He was so perfectly shaped, in a simple matte finish, unassuming, with smooth graceful lines. She gave me the discount she always offers me, bringing the price from $55 to $48. I had no business spending that much money on a porcelain figure just then, but nothing mattered except that I had to own this bunny from Poland.

I told Claire about my recent coincidence with Władek sending family tree information for my birthday and that was part of my conversation in the café just before I got to her shop. She too was startled by the chain of events which ended with me stopping in specifically looking for a bunny and finding one from Poland.

We chatted about Gosia's visit several years before when Gos was charmed by Claire's tea cup collection — her favorite shop in the entire three weeks of her visit to the States.

As I left, Claire asked what I would name the new bunny. I told her I'd think on that one. Maybe it should be Władek. Surprised again, she said, "That's exactly what I was going to suggest!"

I returned home to relate the latest story to Hoot and went straight to my computer to do a Google search for Cybis figurines. Email was open and there was a message from Gosia. She had written after many weeks of being out of touch — moved by my story of Władek's birthday gift which I had sent her. She said she was "Knocked out by what Władek found out, and all the connections including the one in New Hampshire, and oh, how small this world is! And I don't believe it's just because of all the feathers along your way, you must have a good Guardian if not a dozen of them!"

The following morning as I was doing re-runs in my head, I thought, 'I couldn't make up stories like this.' It occurred to me that there was still another coincidence. My mother used to enjoy walking to Claire's shop, to find gifts for me. Claire would help her with the selection and Nana would be so happy to be able to go there independently without asking to be driven.

Furthermore, the day I was born it was the Saturday before Easter and my mother often said I was her Easter bunny. Happenstance, fate, fluke or feathers directed my impulsive visit to Claire's shop that Good Friday afternoon.

Another seeker contacted me by email after seeing my Kolbuszowa pages on Virtual Tourist. Nate Plaza was searching for information on his family from the Kolbuszowa area in Poland, hoping that I might recognize some of his family names. Experience taught me that the first thing to do was verify the spelling of the name. Poles always seem to know the correct spelling of Polish names so you should ask one of them. I forwarded Nate's email to Władek for verification and to ask if the family name was familiar to him. Not only did Władek know the spelling was correct, but he responded to the delight of Nate – that they were related through his mother's family! Incredible. Their email relationship has continued and we all share the delight each time another relative is identified. As the three of us became acquainted, I questioned Nate about where he was located. New Hampshire, he reported. "What part? My son has recently taken a job in New Hampshire and will be moving there with his wife." "I'm in Hudson, just outside Nashua." Christopher's new job was in Nashua and they ultimately moved into a house not more than two miles from Nate. How small the world had become and what fun it was to have connected another family to their roots. Władek's presence on the other end has been such a blessing.

Ancestry.com has been the other vital element helping us to connect the pieces of the puzzle. Grandfather's ship manifest found by the National Archives volunteer in D.C. was not the accurate record. That manifest listed Marcin as 25 years old from "Pajecrzna," arriving in 1908. We had determined there was no such town in Poland and had eliminated the similarly spelled "Pajeczno" as a possibility during our trip in 2001. Repeated searches through Ancestry.com by both Władek and me resulted in his finally discovering the accurate record. It stated Marcin was 27, from Zarębki, Austria (Poland under Austrian rule) who sailed for two weeks and four days from Hamburg to NYC on his way to Webster, Massachusetts to join his brother and cousin. He was listed as married, his brother paid his passage, and he arrived with $7 on hand.

Webster was named in honor of Daniel Webster, the distinguished statesman from Massachusetts. It was a manufacturing town, with its chief products being cotton, woolen goods and thread. As the town's industry expanded, the demand for unskilled labor grew. Poles were immigrating in large numbers. As the Polish settlement in Webster grew they eventually were able to build their own church to serve mass in their newly organized parish. Soon they had paid off the debts of the church, built a school with four Felician Sisters as teachers and by 1906; there were 500 children as students. St. Joseph's was the first Polish American Roman Catholic Parish in New England. No doubt those first parishioners wrote home to Poland to report the success of their church and the need for labor in their new home town.

This Arrival information made more sense, listing Marcin from Zarębki, but the new information stunned me. I wondered why there was never a mention of a brother in the States or the town of Webster. Telephones and computers were not a part of Marcin's world and lacking the ability to write a letter, it's easy to understand how he would drift out of touch with a brother in Massachusetts. But not to have talked to his family about his brother's existence or the first town he lived in when coming to the States, simply confounds me. We always assumed the first stop for the family was in Fall River, Massachusetts where my mother was said to be the first child to be born in the U.S. The family lore was again incorrect. Martin went to Webster in 1905. The cousin mentioned on the manifest would have been Agnes Skowron, mislabeled as his step-sister (later clarified by Gosia as his cousin). All of this led to more searches for the brother who had preceded Martin to the States.

2001 · · · · · 2003 · · · · · 2006 · · · · · 2008 · · · · 2009 · · · ·

Władek knew I struggled with missing pieces to the family puzzle. He occasionally sent copies of documents he found online when he had a little time to search. Amazingly he found records which showed the arrival of Marianna and Piotr, my grandmother and Uncle Peter, coming to join my grandfather in Central Falls, R.I. on February 19, 1909. Marianna, who was listed as 4'9" tall, sailed from Antwerp, Belgium aboard the S.S. Gothland with her three year old son, Piotr, and arrived in NYC with $5. Only Władek could find these missing records which had created so much mystery in the Zosa family. She was no "stow-away." Records were not lost or burned. The truth was that the clerk who hand wrote the ship's manifest had horrible handwriting and had misspelled her name as MARIANNA ZASA. Władek being a Rząsa himself was accustomed to the common misspellings and pronunciations of his name. The later transcription of the ship's manifest for Ancestry.com and other computerized records was further misspelled from the previous bad penmanship, and her name became MARGAR-MANN LARA travelling with PIOTE LARA. No small wonder the National Archives clerks trying to help Uncle Peter with his Naturalization couldn't find these elusive records. If only we had made these discoveries while my mother and her siblings were still alive to dispel some of their suspicions of their parents. In addition to their negative feelings about their alcoholic mother, they might have had some compassion for this little courageous woman who made her way from the tiny village in the hinterlands of Poland, following her husband to a new world.

Soon I was piecing together the larger picture of what was happening in New England with the path of Martin and his family as they started life in the new world. Small details listed in these ship's rosters continued to open further avenues of investigation, leading to more searches for the brother who preceded Martin as well as the towns recorded in their travels.

Central Falls, Rhode Island, where Marianna rejoined her husband, is a one-square-mile town located about 35 miles from Webster, Massachusetts. It has been best symbolized by its ethnic diversity and its religious backgrounds. Around 1890 the Little City was a large producer of various items from brooms and bottles to tools, knitting machines and thread. One of the most important industries of the city was Conant's Mill, later known as Coats Thread Mills, which became so lucrative that three additional buildings were constructed within four years.

With such dynamic growth, the need for laborers to operate the machines grew along with the industry. I remembered Aunt Agnes telling us that Coats & Clark Thread Company was one of the places my grandmother had worked. The growth of this industry dovetailed nicely with the thousands of immigrants pouring into the country from homelands which could no longer support their burgeoning populations.

When all this corrected arrival information came into the mix, it required a slight shift in gears away from the vertical search through the history of New England and Poland to a more horizontal investigation of who was travelling with the Rząsas as well as who was living in the same house or down the street. I was accustomed to adjusting my vision of Marcin's life during this era but discovering he had come to a brother in Webster was another major revelation. Władek and I agreed that I would have to examine a lot more arrival records to get back to the first immigrant from Zarębki who initiated this chain of events. As I examined ships' rosters, I could see a pattern of Rząsa, Skowron and Czeczot families reporting Webster as their destination and Zarębki as their last place of residence.

City directories and census data showed groups of families living together in Central Falls and Fall River. A pattern began to develop which followed the development of those cities. My sources revealed the employment of each member when the census was taken. Threader, spinner, spooler, weaver were common descriptions in these reports. It's more time consuming, but I have learned to view the original documents in Ancestry. com to see details not shown on the transcribed front page. The handwriting is sometimes impossible to decipher, but this is where you glean street addresses, neighbors, occupations, and relationships within a household. You might find brothers or in-laws living with the "head of house" and family. Maiden names can also be discovered this way.

The 1910 Census in Central Falls revealed a group of familiar names living at 28 Charles Street — a house that sheltered 32 people. Kazimierz Czeczot, with wife and son, and Wojciech Czeczot, with wife and 4 children, cohabited with my grandparents Martin, Mary and their son, Peter Rząsa. A 17-year-old Mary Rząsa and 19-year-old Lawrence Skowron were also members of this household group. All of them were working in the "Cotton Mill" at the time.

Wojciech had arrived in 1903, Kazimierz in 1904. Agnieszka Skowron Czeczot joined her husband Wojciech in 1905 along with her 3-year-old daughter, Zofia. Marcin Rząsa sailed with her and her child. In 1907 Agatha Czeczot joined her husband, Kazimierz, arriving with Lawrence Skowron. Mary and Peter Rząsa joined my grandfather in 1909. Living arrangements couldn't have been much better than the crowded little house in Poręby, but the difference was that each member could find work in a mill and there was some promise of a better life.

As both Władek and I poked through these old records, Władek stumbled upon still more information about my grandparents. I had a vague recollection of my mother mentioning a baby lost to her parents, but very little detail was included and I had forgotten the mention of it. Władek found birth and death records for a one year old baby Melina Zasa of Central Falls on October 17, 1911. There was no explanation for the death but we know that babies were frequently lost to simple childhood diseases. The family moved shortly after that and my mother was born in Fall River on January 24, 1912. That means Marianna was six months pregnant, had just lost a one year old, and they somehow made the move (without a car) to Fall River in

time for the next child's birth — in the dead of winter. It makes
me wonder if the death had something to do with the move.
There is another mystery which may never be solved.

The time in Fall River was fairly brief. By 1918, at the age
of 5, my mother had been placed in the state home/orphanage
in Providence. The records do not show Peter or Agnes in the
Home although my mother made the reference using "we."
Peter was 13 years old by then and probably stayed at home.
Agnes would have been two years old but there is no mention
of where she was at that time.

Władek discovered that the year after my mother's institu-
tionalization, there was another baby lost to Marianna. Her son,
Stephen lived only two hours and died in February, 1919. I still
have dark thoughts about these mysteries.

Shifting back to Kolbuszowa and Władek's family farm, I
tried to understand how his family gained ownership of their
property. Władek's wrote:

> "It is a hard question about how people inherited land
> in Galicia. As far as I know women inherited nothing and
> because of that parents were giving them dowry. Sometimes
> it was house stuff or some farm animals like a cow and a few
> chickens. Some rich families were giving them some land but
> not too much (about 1 morga which is 0.5ha).[14]

---

14   A morga is a unit of measurement of land used in Poland, Germany,
Austria and the Netherlands. The size of a morga varied from ½ to 2½ acres,
which equals approximately 0.2 to 1 hectare. It represents the amount of land
tillable by one man behind an ox in the morning hours of the day. The morga
was commonly set at about 60-70% of the "tagwerk" (literally "day work")

"The donation was always made on her name in the notary office before marriage. After Austria took over that land, rules change and all siblings have same rights to inheritance. I have to say it never happened that way. People were always making testament and were giving their kids what they wanted. Sometimes the person would say the farm must be kept in one hand and I don't want to share the land and decision was left for wife to make. Sometimes the person who stayed on main land was keeping 75% of it. That was practiced in my family. If the land owner did not leave testament kids were fighting for their part and all those things were making to split family, keeping them angry to each other and also were making farms small and smaller. My farm at the beginning had 45 ha. And now we have 6 ha.

"In my family things were different. Grandpa did not accept his part of his father's land. He told his sister, "I don't want it." My grand mum, and the farm where we live now she inherited after her father's death and she had to pay money to other 2 brothers and 3rd one was given 25% of farm because he married girl from next door and also she had to pay him money because of repayment of 25% of farm buildings. Everything was different in each family. The thing is that Galicia was such a poor area with such small farms that people were leaving to go to the US to look for a better place to live or find a place where they could survive. In Galicia with such a big population it was hard to live. Parents tried to be fair but how to share 3 ha [hectare] farm for 8 people. There is no way to do it. People who stayed at farm and weren't a land owner became farmhands and their material status was more than poor. Some parents were afraid to make a donation to their kids before they die because many old people

---

referring to a full day of ploughing.

Władek reported the morga used in Kolbuszowa area was an Austrian version equal to half a hectare, or approximately 1.25 acres.

---

were treated as an extra person to feed and many of them were banished, became beggars. That was the reason that testaments were more popular than a donation.

"The farm is now on my parents name and they have proper ownership. ...The situation with my farm was difficult because the system we had before 1989. My grand mum went to the court in a wrong time and that is what messed everything. Government didn't know what they want to do with private property, and my grand mum was left with property which wasn't register in her name. The communistic government did many things like that and we all are spending money to fix it.

"We were lucky because grandma had old ownership certificate from her dad and that helped..... Government cancelled register when she inherited the farm, so she thought they would do it again, but the register from 1970 is now the one which is valid. If you have old ownership before war you may fight for it and win but it takes time and money. We were lucky because it took us a year to fix it.

"About your grandpa, I think the reason he left to US was because of their situation. Their house was full, and he was the youngest with no chance to get anything. The reason why he may have stopped contact with his family could be, and I'm sure for 100% that was money. He left there many poor people without chance for better life. All families have same stories, even mine."

Sixth Trip to Poland

Krakow

◈

Rzeszow

◈

Kolbuszowa

◈

Cmolas

◈

Zarębki

◈

Mechowiec

◈

Poręby Dymarskie

Years passed, as did my husband. I scaled down my work life. There was more time to think of Poland, Władek, and the continuous flow of seekers with roots in Kolbuszowa who found me on my Virtual Tourist pages on the internet. Of all the thousands of contributors to Virtual Tourist.com, I was the creator of pages on Kolbuszowa, Cmolas, Zarębki and Poręby Dymarskie. Google searches by descendants of Polish immigrants would find photos and stories of my travels through the hinterlands of Poland and write to tell me about their connection to that rural corner of the world. Some seekers were planning a trip to Poland and had lots of questions about my time there, while others I referred to Władek to check the spelling of names or we'd give direction as they began their search which was all so familiar to me. Writing the story of my family and the search for grandfather's village consumed much of my attention. The story could continue for years as we found more details about the Rząsa history as well as other Rząsa families trying to connect to mine.

Health issues reduced my confidence to travel but I longed for another opportunity to be enveloped by Poland's special aura, energy and warmth. And so I determined that I must journey across those many miles to Kolbuszowa once again, and write the final chapter of my story on the farm in Poręby Dymarskie – the land once owned by one of my ancestors. It was my link to Władek's family, who still farmed and lived at #35.

A few glorious days were spent in Krakow with dear Gosia who still tolerates me and continues her enthusiasm with my book, taking on the task of Polish Editor. Władek arrived with Gary and Shirley (seekers from Connecticut I had connected to Władek who were in Kolbuszowa and Cmolas the previous week). Research escapades were reviewed, archives were visited,

and we chattered and ate until it was time for everyone to go
their separate ways.

Total Immersion

Władek and I drove the newer roads to Kolbuszowa and the
four year old hotel built since my last visit – a welcome addition
to the community. I noticed many changes, improvements and
modernizations along the way – with each of my visits Poland
grows, changes and evolves.

After dropping my luggage, we drove to see Władek's parents on the farm. We took a different route but I had a general
idea of where I was, which seemed strange that I was so familiar
with this foreign territory. When Władek led me back to the
hotel at the end of the day, I could recount all the guideposts
along the way; I was certain I could drive it by myself without
getting lost, and the following night, I did.

The warmest hugs greeted me at the Rząsa farm. Once again
I was struck by the familiarity of Władek's father (Mieczysław,
or the more familiar "Mieciu") as he engaged with me – speaking as if I understood his language, and there are times when
I do. The context and hand gestures, tone of voice and general
"knowingness" of common activities and situations helps to
convey the thoughts if you pay close enough attention and he
seems to know that I do.

Maria is always busy with feeding, cooking or running out to do another farm chore. She's a small woman who usually has a house dress covering her clothes and a knitted hat on her head. I know she's very strong, but she appears gentle and delicate. Her energy never seems to wane as she sets the pace for the day's activities.

We visited over lunch (even though Władek and I had just eaten) and I gave them the gifts I had brought from the States. Mieciu (Władek's father) was especially intrigued with the wood plane I brought from my friend, Ned. Taking it apart and testing the sharpness of the blade, his concentration was exclusive to the token from America.

Mieciu and Maria Rzasa

At my request for a tour, we moved without delay to the barn. Mieciu had enlarged the space since my last visit, leaving the original old beams pegged by an ancestor as the interior skeleton. Hay was piled high for winter, dogs barked and jumped, chickens scurried, the cows looked mournful with tagged ears and the pigs were happy in their filth. Everything was reviewed as each outbuilding was explored. We finally came to the wood shop. Confusion and dust were all around but Mieciu knew where his special wood tools were and he climbed on a bench to bring his favorites down for me to see. There were one after another homemade wood planes of various description, size and purpose. This one his father's, that one his grandfather's — all of them hand made by the farmer for his own peculiar need.

He loves showing me his projects and equipment, reporting the age of things and grinning when I react to all of it. I know he enjoys my visit. His hands and body are powerful — his face aged by sun and wind, but the Polish blue eyes are soft, merry, kind.

I watched the interaction of farmer and wife who needed no discussion about the afternoon chores and soon they climbed onto an old tractor pulling a large wooden wagon. They disappeared for a while and returned with a wagon filled with tall grasses which Mieciu carried in to the cows that were waiting for their scheduled 2nd feeding of the day.

There is a simple rhythm between Maria and Mieciu from years of moving in time to nature. I found it beautiful.

We made a plan for me to return to the farm on Saturday for the slaughter of the pig and making kielbasa. They joked that I would hold the pig's leg while Mieciu slayed the animal, but they knew full well I would not have enough farmer genes in me to take part in such a procedure. We share our laughter which needs no common language.

I planned my morning so that the bloodletting would be finished by the time I got to the farm. Władek, his parents, and Ola[15] were well into the butchering process by the time I arrived. Five gallon pots atop an old wood burning stove held

---

15   Ola is Władek's sister-in-law, living on the farm while her husband, Bogdan works in Belgium.

boiling liquids and pig parts, creating bouillon and ingredients for blood sausage, paté, and "jelly." They took particular delight tying a cotton scarf around my head. "Babushka!" they laughed and all agreed I looked very Polish. There was a tempo to the work of the day which continued without a lunch break as everyone moved around the "summer kitchen" housed in an outbuilding behind the house. Two people were always at the butchering table while alternating tasks kept the process moving in perfect orchestration. Bacon was seasoned and marinated before smoking. Heart, lungs and kidney were separated, boiled and used to grind with buckwheat creating a 4-inch round sausage which Maria would later slice and fry as she needed it. The stove had to be fed to keep the fire strong.

Maria shoos the cat out of the workspace. The grinder was brought from storage. Mieciu produced a wooden wheel to form a belt-driven system to electrify the grinder, eliminating a tedious part of the job. There are many similar adaptations around the farm, which Mieciu has invented to make their work easier. I was fascinated by the choreography of the day as I watched the sorting, mixing, grinding and smoking of the final products. I couldn't have found a better way to understand my grandfather's life in Poland than to be with these people who enveloped me into their family.

I got to drive the tractor and ride in the grass-filled wagon through fields and forests. I opened the gates for Maria to walk the cows to a nearby field. We sat in the crowded corner of the kitchen snacking on meats, potato pancakes and Maria's home-made plum cake. We laughed a lot in those days on the farm and I found I enjoyed my lack of Polish as I became proficient in the language of humanity. There were so many wonderful moments but the underlying joy of being part of that pure, uncontaminated family farmland could never be adequately conveyed. I feel privileged to be considered part of this family now. I know why I am who I am and it feels comfortable. It gives me peace.

Janet and Miccin

Throughout my visit Władek kept the focus on our research. We visited archives in Kraków, Rzeszów and Kolbuszowa to find hamlet maps dating back to the 1700s; we spoke with neighbors on the street where the Rząsa family lived, including Mrs. Kapusta (now 97 years old) who we visited previously. We found the street where grandmother grew up. Cemeteries in Mechowiec and Cmolas had to be explored and photographed. Finally we went to our scheduled appointment with the new priest in Cmolas. Father Matthew is a very young priest with enormous patience and a serenity which permeated the room. He poured over the old volumes with Władek until they had culled every piece of available information about the Fieluba and Rząsa clans all the way back to the earliest books in the church, which brought us to the 1700s. Władek has become so proficient in these searches that he often guides the priest in the fastest way to find every possible entry. The process continued for two and a half hours. We found birth, marriage, death dates and house numbers for three generations prior to my grandparents, including many of their siblings. One story stood out in this exploration and that was the family history of my grandmother, Marianna Fieluba Rząsa. Władek had persisted in finding evidence which might help explain her behavior in later years. He once said he didn't make excuses for her, but understood the loneliness of the immigrant forced to leave their homeland because there was no work available. His insight is that of a young man who himself has migrated to London to find work. He seemed to identify with my grandparents' life journey.

Marianna (grandmother) Fieluba's parents were married when Antoni was 38 and Apolonia was 22. Marianna was their first born in March of 1882. A second daughter (Katarzyna) was born in 1883. Antoni died in 1889 when my grandmother was just 7 years old. Marianna's sister Katarzyna died at nearly seven years old in 1890. Apolonia then gave birth to an "illegitimate" daughter who died within her first year in 1890. A few years later in 1893 another daughter, Ewa, was born out of wedlock and after searching the records all the way up to 1918, there was no information found about her life, marriage, or death. We concluded she was still alive when Marianna left Poland. This is as much as we could discover about my grandmother's formative years before she married Marcin. The data presented a rather gloomy childhood. Władek later asked if I would bring this new information to my Uncle Michael when I got home. He said, "Maybe it would help him understand." I wasn't sure I would or if I did, how successful such an effort would be.

I later thought about that difficult childhood followed by a marriage that was suspended while grandfather left to find a new life in America. She had years of sad nights as she waited for him to send for her and her son, Peter, as they lived in an overcrowded house on the street I visited in Zarębki. The steerage accommodations on the long voyage to America were probably worse, and then she was stuffed into overcrowded tenement houses while working the New England thread mills. I'm not so mystified about her abusive drinking although it's hard to forgive some of her extreme behavior. We'll never know when or what made her stop drinking. Maybe once her family was grown and she had become accustomed to life in Providence, she was able to find peace in the loyalty of her husband – that lovely little quiet man who smiled with her when they saw those silly little girls peering in the window of their Providence home. I am still that silly child reveling in my Polish heritage and hoping my story brings understanding and peace to others.

As Sunday approached, Władek told me there was a 10:30am mass at the old church in Poręby Dymarskie. I should get there by 10:00am if I was to get a seat, so I was there at the prescribed hour but the church was already full. I sat in the back of the church on a narrow wooden bench surrounded by the people of Poręby Dymarskie chanting the rosary before mass began. It's a remarkable sound and custom. There are no brief genuflections by the people of this parish. Everyone gets down on both knees to pray before taking their seat. Older women surprise me with their agility.

As one small boy walks past with his mother, I imagine my grandfather as an altar boy with white frock moving candles and crosses or holding mama's hand on the way up the aisle.

The paintings, statues and crucifixes are extraordinary in this 15th century church which has been relocated and restored by the men of this hamlet. It's so awe-inspiring that words fail me. The story of these farmers using primitive tools and oxen to move the church which would become the heart of their village is seldom told, yet remarkable. Władek's grandfather was one of those dedicated men; a man who farmed the land Władek's father farms today and my ancestors farmed in the 1800s. It's all a part of my blood line.

My journey came to an end filled with joyful memories and gratitude for all the people who became part of my pilgrimage to grandfather's village. It's been forty years since my first passage into the environs of Eastern Europe. Years filled with digging, discovering, learning and laughter. I could never have imagined that I would learn about the Rząsa lineage in such depth – or that there would be such incredible people to help me on my path. My endeavor sprung from the depths of my soul without awareness of where it would lead me. There has been a dogged determination to continue which seemed to accelerate after each family member's demise, making me feel as if I was racing against a universal clock. It has felt like a mission to uncover and document the life of my grandfather; to understand that diminutive unvarnished man, his family and homeland.

When Gosia read a draft of my manuscript she said, "Just to realize you started quite in the dark and ended up finding your relatives still living on your grandmother's family's land is almost unbelievable. Władek was a godsend. If I hadn't been involved in this search, I would think you've made it all up!"

I'm glad I persisted, found the true family name, corrected family misconceptions, and uncovered the truth about the Rząsa's early years in the United States. I hope the list of books and resources I poured through will give other seekers inspiration and direction. I feel as if I've tidied up a lot of loose ends and stacked everything in its proper place. Not only is there now a record of Marcin Rząsa and his family, but it's more accurate than what we grew up with.

Friends ask what inspired my search and I'm at a loss to construct a well-turned-out explanation. The entire odyssey has been driven by the same instinct and enthusiasm Hoot and I shared on our trek into the unknown on our first trip to Warsaw in 1974. I am so thankful for every facet of my adventure. The story of the Rząsa/Zosa family isn't unique. It's a story that resembles thousands of others, but it's my grandfather's and it's mine.

Epilogue

Susan Nora Hartman

Our lives are made up of so many threads over time. Sometimes they intertwine tightly, or separate and drift, but always they connect us one to the other. It seems that over my whole life I've watched my mother search for the ways in which the threads of our Polish family are tied together as if that fabric would finally tell a story. As I read her manuscript, it was like opening drawers with memories I had forgotten, about experiences I had been involved with and known about since I was an early teen. The bits and pieces of this story came at so many different points over time that it didn't occur to me how they were strung together, until I read this story in its completion. My mother has always been one of singular purpose and in her search to connect the family story back to the beginning she has never wavered. Through her journey I have been an inadvertent participant and guide, occasionally helping her link to places where she searched, and being a not-too-distant observer in how this mystery unfolded. It was sometimes unclear to me what drove her to seek this information out and why it meant so much. Until we made that trip to Poland together. And then it was like magic. Or at least it seemed so to me.

Perhaps it was the experience of being in Poland at a critical time in US history, or just the full immersion in the culture for so many days, but being in this beautiful country and meeting its warm, generous people made it very real. And it was following that trip that doors continued to unlock in constant succession for her. Perhaps it's a bit metaphysical to see it this way, but her seeking, and finding, and making the family story real, seems to have brought healing and light into a place that was so dark and unknown. And recognizing her strong and honest heart, the universe finally rewarded her with the many Polish angels that have helped her on her way. It was as if someone opened the door and said "It's time for you to know. Welcome, we've been waiting for you."

Sources and Readings

Ash, Timothy Garton, *The Polish Revolution: Solidarity*, 2002, Yale University Press

Brandys, Kazimierz, *A Question of Reality: A Novel of Poland*, 1980, Free Press

Chorzempa, Rosemary A., *Polish Roots*, 1993, Genealogical Publishing Co., Inc.

Colletta, Ph.D., John P., *They Came In Ships*, 1989, Ancestry.com

Curie, Madame, (Translated by Vincent Sheean), *Madame Curie: A Biography*, 1937, Da Capo Press: A Member of the Perseus Books Group

Davies, Norman, *Rising '44: The Battle for Warsaw*, 2004, Penguin Publishing Group

Dolar, Sean, *The Polish Americans*, 1997, Chelsea House Publishers

Draus, Ph.D., Jan, *Ziemia Kolbuszowska*, 2000, Księgarnia Akademicka LIBRA

Drakulic, Slavenka, *Café Europa: Life After Communism*, 1996, Penguin Publishing Group

Halperin, Jonathan J., *The Other Side: How Soviets and Americans Perceive Each Other*, 1991, Transaction Publishers

Hoffman, Eva, *Exit Into History: A Journey Through the New Eastern Europe*, 1993, Faber and Faber

Kazik (Rotem, Sionha), *Kazik: Memories of a Warsaw Ghetto Fighter*, 1994, Yale University Press

Kelly, Eric P., *The Trumpeter of Krakow*, 1928, Aladdin (2012)

Kosicki, C.S.B., George W., *Revelations of Divine Mercy*, 1996, Francisco Media

Lanckorońska, Countess Karolina, *Those Who Trespass Against Us: One Woman's War Against the Natzis*, 2006, Pimlico

Libeskind, Daniel, *Breaking Ground*, 2004, Penguin Group

Lutz, Aloysius A. & Richard J. Lutz, *Jadwiga's Crossing*, 2006, iUniverse, Inc.

Majhewski, Karen, *Traitors & True Poles*, 2003, Ohio University Press

Meacham, Jon, *Franklin and Winston: An Intimate Portrait of an Epic Friendship*, 2004, Random House Publishing Group

Michener, James A., *Poland*, 1983, Random House Publishing Group

Reymont, Ladislas, *The Peasants: A Tale of Our Times in Four Volumes: Spring*, 1925, Alfred Knopf

Rosenberg, Tina, *The Haunted Land*, 1996, Knopf Doubleday

Stauter-Halsted, Keely, *The Nation in the Village: The Genesis of Peasant National Identity in Austrian Poland 1848-1914*, 2001, Cornell University Press

Salsitz, Norman, *A Jewish Boyhood in Poland: Remembering Kolbuszowa*, 1999, Syracuse University Press

Silorska, Grazyab, *Jerzy Popietusko: A Martyr For the Truth*, 1984, Alphascript Publishing

Sieradzka, Anna, *Poland's Living Folk Culture*, 2004, Parma Press

Walesa, Lech, *Walesa A Way of Hope: An Autobiography*, 1987, Holt, Henry & Company

Wallner, Rosemary, *Coming to America: Polish Immigrants 1890-1920*, 2003, Capstone Press

Weschler, Lawrence, *Poland in the Season of its Passion*, 1982, Knopf Doubleday

Wiegel, George, *Witness To Hope: The Biography of Pope John Paul II*, 2001, Harper Collins Publishers

Zamoyski, Adam, *The Polish Way! A Thousand-year History of the Poles and Their Culture*, 1987, Scholastic Library Publishing

Znaniecki, Florian and William I. Thomas, *The Polish Peasant in Europe and America: A Classic Work in Immigration History*, 1996, University of Illinois Press

www.Delphi.com (Message Boards)

www.Ancestry.com

www.RandomActsofGenealogicalKindness.com

Ellis Island NYC & Ellis Island online

Social Security Death Index

City of Hamburg Immigration Records online

Journal Newspaper, November 27, 1994, Neighborhoods: South Central Falls
   Historic District by David Traub

Family Research Center Church of Latter Day Saints, Warwick, R.I.

National Archives, Woburn, Mass.

National Archives, Washington, D.C.

Dept. of Justice, Immigration & Naturalization Service, 950 Pennsylvania
   Ave., Wash., D.C.

RI Historic Society Library, 121 Hope St., Prov., R.I.

Woonsocket Library, 303 Clinton St., Woonsocket, R.I.

The Polish Museum of America, 984 N. Milwaukee Ave. Chicago, Ill.

R.I. College – DCYF & Superintendent's Cottage, 600 Mt. Pleasant Ave.,
   Providence, R.I.

St. Stanislaw Church, 36 Rockland St., Fall River, Mass.

Asbury United Methodist Church, 143 Ann Mary Brown D., Warwick, R.I.

Diocese of Providence Archives, 1 Cathedral Square, Providence, R.I.

St. Adalbert's Church, 866 Atwells Ave., Providence, R.I.

Blackstone River State Park, State of Rhode Island Department of
   Environmental Management, 235 Promenade St., Providence, R.I.

Blackstone River Valley Map, National Park Service, U.S. Department of the
   Interior, Providence, R.I. & 1849 C. St. N.W. Washington, DC